ONE PEOPLE

עם אחד

Publication of this volume was made possible
by a grant from The Memphis-Plough Charitable
Trust in memory of Moses and Julia Plough

ONE PEOPLE

A Study in Comparative Judaism

ABRAHAM SEGAL

Edited by

BERNARD M. ZLOTOWITZ

Union of American Hebrew Congregations

New York, New York

Library of Congress Cataloging in Publication Data

Segal, Abraham, 1910-1977
    One people.

    Summary: Describes the similarities and differences among the
three branches of Judaism while emphasizing the ties which bind all
Jews together as a people. Includes exercises, questions, and activities.
    1. Judaism—20th century—Juvenile literature. 2. Judaism—
United States—Juvenile literature 3. Jews—United States—Politics
and government—Juvenile literature. [1. Judaism] I. Zlotowitz, Ber-
nard M. II. Title.
BM105.S44 1982   296.8'3'0973   82–17633
ISBN 0–8074–0169–2

IN MEMORIAM
ABRAHAM SEGAL
1910—1977

Who among all people are the most beloved and lovely? One of our sages responded: It is those teachers who teach children faithfully for they will sit at God's right hand.

Such a faithful teacher was Abraham Segal. He taught not only children and young people. Abe was a teacher of teachers. His was a life devoted to study, to learning, to the transmittal of knowledge and Jewish values. He sought to ensure the highest quality of education, expressing the great ideals and teachings of our faith in such a fashion as to affect Jewish lives and Jewish commitment. Abe sought to nourish the inner being of his students as well as their minds.

A lifelong educator, Abe's career climaxed in his service as Director of the Joint Commission on Jewish Education of the Union of American Hebrew Congregations and the Central Conference of American Rabbis. In his great devotion and dedication to quality Jewish education, Abe sought always to enrich and enhance Jewish learning and experience on every level of congregational life—from preschool to adult years. His own creativity in writing culminated in the magnificent volume *Israel Today,* a loving tribute to the Jewish state, which has become a classic and his living legacy to the future, and, of course, in this volume, *One People,* his final work.

Zecher tzadik livrachah—The memory of Abraham Segal will remain for a blessing.

RABBI ALEXANDER M. SCHINDLER, President
Union of American Hebrew Congregations

July, 1982

FOREWORD

Abraham Segal was a giant in Jewish education. Though he never sought public acclaim, his colleagues revered him as a visionary thinker, a brilliant teacher, and a gentle and supportive mentor to whom they could always turn for sound advice, encouragement, and creative solutions to virtually any problem.

Generations of Jewish children, past and present, were also blessed by Abraham Segal's genius. *Israel Today,* which he co-authored, still stands as the single finest textbook on the Jewish state. And the methodology embodied in his countless teacher's guides and articles still finds expression in the Jewish classrooms of North America today.

One People is part of Abraham Segal's legacy to the future. It captures his love for *K'lal Yisrael* and his insistence that Jews of all movements can grow together, respecting differences in ideology and practice, but always emphasizing the ties that bind us together as a people.

We express our thanks to those individuals who, as a labor of love, took the rough drafts and notes which Abe left at the time of his passing and shaped them into this volume:

Rabbi Bernard Zlotowitz,
> Abe's collaborator and friend, who helped to develop the book, edited it with care, and served as the single greatest advisor to the rewriting team.

Rabbi Leonard Schoolman,
> who penned two additional chapters on current concerns.

Steven Schnur and Josette Knight,
  who revised and strengthened the final manuscript.
Annette Daum, Sadie Segal, and Rabbi Steven Reuben,
  who read the text at various stages and made many
  helpful comments and suggestions.
Eppie Begleiter, who typed the final manuscript.
And Stuart Benick, UAHC Director of Publications,
  who supervised the book's production.
  We hope that you will use and enjoy *One People* as part
of your growth as a Jew. We are proud to share it with you.

DANIEL B. SYME
Director of Education

EDITOR'S INTRODUCTION

The idea for this book began to germinate in Abraham Segal's mind over three decades ago. During that period he collected data, newspaper clippings, magazine articles, stories, and poems with the intention of writing an exciting book about American Judaism. He believed that a textbook instead of listing facts (which could be easily obtained in any good encyclopedia) should challenge the minds of both the teacher and the student. Together they would probe and examine, understand and appreciate the major differences and the finer subtleties that distinguish the different branches of Judaism—Reform, Orthodox, Conservative, and Reconstructionist. In this book he achieved his goal.

Abe did not live to complete *One People;* nevertheless, his spirit permeates this book and his ideas are imprinted on every page. Since I worked closely with him on this volume and supervised the field testing of the preliminary sections in religious schools, I was invited by Rabbi Daniel Syme, Abe's worthy successor as director of education, to edit and complete the manuscript. In addition to my efforts, Rabbi Syme and Rabbi Leonard Schoolman contributed important chapters.

In the process of writing the book, Abe and I tested his concepts in two religious schools among students in the Bar/Bat Mitzvah and pre-Confirmation grades, difficult grades where many students show a lack of interest in Jewish study, often claiming that "it's boring." When we introduced the first part of the book, the classroom came alive as students sought to fathom their Jewishness within the totality of *am echad* (one people). To the delight of parents and teachers, absenteeism dropped to its lowest level in years.

A word of caution: Often there are no right or wrong answers. The questions merely serve to challenge, to help students begin to explore Judaism for themselves. If this be accomplished then this book is a fitting tribute, a *zikaron olam,* to the memory of Abraham Segal, educational innovator, profound thinker, educator par excellence, friend, and a man with a beautiful soul.

BERNARD M. ZLOTOWITZ

CONTENTS

UNIT I

Don't Jump to Conclusions!
Come Let's Reason Together

The first unit of this book is purposely designed to confuse you about the three largest branches of Judaism—Reform, Orthodox, and Conservative Judaism. We want to show you how hard it is, sometimes, to tell them apart. That means putting you through some real challenges.

But don't get upset. One good way to really learn something is to get so involved that you want to master it. Actually, you can have lots of fun with this unit.

Are you willing to match wits with me for a while and be patient until we find some solid answers?

ROUND ONE

Warm-up

Think this one over—as a class, in small groups, or by yourself. Then write out your own brief answers.

The main difference between Reform, Conservative, and Orthodox Jews is:

_____

Other important differences are:

1. _____
2. _____
3. _____

4. _____

5. _____

R Now tackle this problem (class, yourself, small groups). Think, talk to people, do some reading first if you like—then write out your answers.

Watch out for traps—and be ready to give the reasons for your answers.

_____

_____

_____

_____

> One of these three Jewish families
> is Reform, one is Conservative, one
> is Orthodox. Which is which?

Chanah and Ari Alef keep kosher at home and away; will not eat bacon or ham; attend synagogue regularly, which they call a "synagogue." Ari Alef wears a yarmulke (skullcap) there. They do not work on Shabbat. They strongly support the State of Israel. Their synagogue's religious school requires every child eight years and older to attend three days a week.

Sarah and Benjamin Bet do not keep kosher anywhere. They attend synagogue, which they call the "temple," only on the High Holy Days of Rosh Hashanah and Yom Kippur and on the Sabbath near *yahrzeit* (anniversary of the death of a next of kin). They work on Shabbat. Both strongly

support Israel. Their son, on the Shabbat afternoon following his Bar Mitzvah, took his friends to a bowling alley and
served pizza.

Rachel and David Gimel keep kosher at home to ac-
commodate their elderly parents, but not away from home.
He wears a yarmulke in synagogue, which he attends fairly
often. Both sometimes work on Shabbat. Their daughter
attends a Jewish day school, where she studies regular public
school subjects and Jewish subjects every day.

Stage 1

These are three real families, whom I know personally. Put
your (Hebrew letters) alef-bet-gimel in the blanks.
1. The Reform Jewish family is____because _____
2. The Conservative Jewish family is____because _____
3. The Orthodox Jewish family is____because _____
Made up your mind?
Then try the next stage.

Stage 2

Put your (Hebrew letters) alef-bet-gimel in the blanks. (The
numbers below the blanks are your keys to the answers given
later.)

The_____family says the_____family's synagogue resembles¹a church.

The_____ family says the other two families' synagogues are foreign to the American way of life.

The_____family says the other two families' synagogues are becoming more like their synagogue all the time.

The_____family claims theirs is the true Judaism
for modern, intelligent Jews.

All right, want to go back now and change your answers
for Stage 1?

Stage 3

Compare your answers and your reasons. Then take a class poll
and fill in what the majority of the class decided:

1. The Reform Jewish family is_____because _____
2. The Conservative Jewish family is_____because _____
3. The Orthodox Jewish family is_____because_____

Stage 4
Now read on and see who's right!

Answers to Round One

Stage 1: Actually, in real life, Mr. and Mrs. Alef are Reform,
Mr. and Mrs. Bet are Conservative, and Mr. and Mrs.
Gimel are Orthodox.
How did you do on this? The class?

Stage 2: Actually, in real life, the filled-in blanks go like this:
1. The Gimel family (Orthodox).
2. The Alef family (Reform).
3. The Alef family (Reform).
4. All three families.
5. All three families.
How did you do on this one? The class?

Got them all right? Some of them? None of them?

Either way, we've got a shock for you about Round
One: There are no right answers!

The whole thing was a trap. Unless you just wanted to
take a random guess, the best answer, in every case, should
have been: "I don't know."

Let's take it step by step.

Fact No. 1: The Alef, Bet, and Gimel families are real
people—but everything I told you about each family could

fit more than one type of Jew. (*Example:* Some Reform Jews keep kosher, some Conservative and Orthodox Jews do not.)

Fact No. 2: Reform Jews differ widely among themselves, in beliefs and practices. Some Reform Jews resemble some Conservative Jews in their beliefs and practices. Conservative Jews also differ widely among themselves. Some behave pretty much like some Reform Jews, others pretty much like some Orthodox Jews. Orthodox Jews, in turn, are far from being all alike. Some of them follow certain Conservative and even Reform practices—though they won't often admit it.

Fact No. 3: Reform, Conservative, and Orthodox Jews are all alike in some ways. Before you can really tell them apart, you have to know such things as:

- which similarities are important and which are not;
- which differences are important and which are not;
- everything each group does and believes—not just some of it;
- what they claim they do—and what they really do;
- what they claim they believe—and what they really believe;
- why they behave and believe as they do—out of conviction, habit, social or family pressures, knowledge, ignorance, and so on.

All of which means that, if you fell into my little trap, you were making one or more of these mistakes:

- you were just guessing;
- you were following a little picture in your mind (we call it a "stereotype") of a Reform, Conservative, or Orthodox Jew—a picture that could be all wrong, mostly wrong, or partly wrong as compared with the actual facts;
- you were jumping to conclusions about all Reform, all Conservative, and all Orthodox Jews from what

you happen to know about some of them. (We call this "faulty generalization.")

Which error were you guilty of—guessing, stereotypes, or faulty generalizations? All three maybe?

ROUND TWO

Warm-up

Write here what you think of a Jew who says:
1. "As a Reform Jew, there's nothing I must do or believe
   —it's all up to me what I do or believe."
   Your response:

   _____

   _____

2. "I'm Conservative, but I don't keep kosher."
   Your response:

   _____

   _____

3. "I'm not very observant, but on holidays I like to go to
   an Orthodox synagogue because I like the atmosphere
   and the *chazan.*"
   Your response:

   _____

   _____

R Alright, now that you know some of the traps
and problems of defining Reform, Conserva-
tive, and Orthodox Judaism, let's try again.
The rules are: don't guess; don't fall for
stereotypes; don't generalize.
Consider the following three statements.
   A Reform rabbi: "We have a secret weapon that could
      turn Conservative Jews into Reform Jews overnight.
      All we Reform Jews have to do is start wearing yar-
      mulkes."
   A Conservative rabbi: "The trouble is not that we have
      Reform, Conservative, and Orthodox Jews—but that

the Orthodox are not really Orthodox; the Conservative, not really Conservative; the Reform, not really Reform."

An Orthodox rabbi: "Conservative congregations provide Orthodox worship for Reform Jews."

Each statement implies certain ideas that the speaker believes but doesn't put openly into words. (We call these "assumptions.") We're going to list some of these assumptions for you and, if you like, you can add others that you figure out for yourself.

Your job: Write YES or NO beside each assumption to show whether or not you agree with it.

———— The only real differences separating the three kinds of Jews are in relatively minor matters of customs and observances.

———— Most Jews don't really know why they call themselves Reform, Conservative, or Orthodox; they don't really know how the three groups differ or what makes their own group distinctive; they don't really practice what their rabbi preaches.

———— In each of the three groups there are sincere, intelligent, dedicated Jews—and also in each of the three groups there are hypocritical, ignorant, indifferent Jews.

———— The Jewishly informed people in all three groups are more like each other—and the Jewishly ignorant people in all three groups are more alike—than Reform Jews are as a group, or Conservative as a group, or Orthodox as a group.

———— Orthodox Judaism is more honest—the others represent compromise, hypocrisy, hunting for easy ways out.

———— Reform Judaism is more honest—Conservative Jews follow Reform practices but don't want to admit it.

_____ Conservative Judaism is more honest—it has decided very definitely what Orthodox practices to keep and what to change.

Work out the majority answers of the whole class and list them beside your own in a separate column. How closely do you conform? Does it matter? Are these the kinds of assumptions that most people make, accept, or disagree with? What was the purpose of this little game, anyhow—to get the "right" assumptions or to recognize and admit your own particular assumptions?

Disappointed? No answers, traps, errors? Don't worry, there'll be more.

Meanwhile—something to do, to round out all this think-tank stuff.

Break up into four groups.

Group A interviews your rabbi to find out about any of these questions—or all of them:

· Why most Reform Jews don't want to wear a yarmulke and why some do?

· What percentage of your congregation's members originally came from a Conservative or Orthodox background—and what problems, if any, this creates?

· Why some synagogues have changed from Reform to Conservative, or from Conservative to Orthodox—or the other way around?

· How do people starting a new synagogue decide whether to be Reform, Conservative, or Orthodox?

Group B—for a real challenge—puts the very same

questions to a Conservative or an Orthodox rabbi (changing the wording a bit as needed).

Group C asks your congregation's president or other top officer about the idea of trying to merge Reform and Conservative Jews into one group.

· Is it a good idea?
· What are the advantages and disadvantages?
· Is it possible?
· What steps would have to be taken and who would have to take them?
· How would a "merged" synagogue operate in worship, religious school, and on holidays?
· What would it be called ("Reformative," "Conservaform," or any other)?

Group D sees your principal about how the school curriculum, from kindergarten through high school, provides for a good understanding of (1) Reform Judaism and (2) "basic" Judaism, the "common core" that makes all Jews part of one "family."

When all four groups are ready, Groups A and B should join to discuss and compare what they found, Groups C and D join for the same purpose. Decide whether you then want to put all four groups together for a general class discussion and what single topic or question would such a discussion deal with.

> Every synagogue—Reform, Conservative, Orthodox—can follow its own beliefs and practices instead of any official national policy. Good or bad?

ROUND THREE

Warm-up

A hard one this time!

Make up some questions of your own about Jews or Judaism, according to the following instructions (you don't have to know the answer):

1. A question that could be answered only by guessing.

---

2. A question that could be answered by a stereotype.

---

3. A question that could lead someone into faulty generalization.

---

4. A question that should be answered with "I don't know."

---

5. A question that could be answered out of real knowledge of all the required facts.

When you compare questions with other students, do not think about the answers—only about whether the questions followed the instructions.

Purpose: To train yourself to think about a question you ask, or a question someone asks you, before you think about the answer. You see, some questions are quite simple, easy to answer, and get most people to agree. But not so with other questions like—

Only a small fraction of the iceberg shows above water and the big, dangerous part of it is invisible down under. With questions like that, you have to look for the down-under part before you try to "navigate" them.

R This time, remember that "don't know" is also an answer—if you think you're not getting enough information, or if the information you're getting could fit more than one type of Jew. Try not to guess, follow a stereotype (those little pictures in your mind), or assume that all Jews are like the ones you know (faulty generalization).

Following are some statements and decisions made by a number of contemporary rabbis.

Decide for each one whether the rabbi is Reform, Conservative, or Orthodox and put R, C, or O in the blank line to indicate your answer. To avoid giving you any hints, all of the statements we've quoted are from male rabbis, even though there are many women rabbis today. If you like, jot down your personal reaction to each rabbi's statement and, maybe, your reasons too—or at least think about your own reaction and your reasons.

_____ Rabbi A shocked many people by saying that God may not be all-powerful.

_____ Rabbi B calls branches of Judaism other than his own "deviate, ersatz (fake) Judaism, inauthentic." He demands an "all-out offensive and manifesto" against them. He insists that all marriages performed by the other branches are not valid.

_____ Rabbi C: "Judaism bases its entire raison d'être (reason for existence) upon a belief in a personal Deity who created us in His own image and who revealed a code of ethics and ritual to determine how the Jewish people shall condition their lives."

_____ Rabbi D: "The Bible (as the book itself makes clear) was not written only for the generations at Mt. Sinai; it was presented as a code for all generations."

_____ Rabbi E sees no need for God in Jewish life. His congregation has eliminated the word and the idea from its prayers and from its religious school. His branch of Judaism has not disowned or expelled him.

_____ Rabbi F refuses to meet with rabbis or educators of the other two branches for any purpose, saying: "If I join them on any project, it would look as if I approve of their kind of Judaism."

_____ Rabbi G calls the official prayer book of his own group "primitive, irrational, infantile—full of anthropomorphisms and sexist language referring to God as father, king, shepherd, and so on."

_____ Rabbi H accuses Orthodox Judaism of not interpreting Jewish tradition to make it apply to contemporary problems like relationships between Jews and non-Jews, the role of women in religious life, and criticisms of religion raised by modern thought.

_____ Rabbi I: "Judaism must become an integral part of the American fabric."

_____ Rabbi J forces the caterer who serves the synagogue to refuse all new year's eve parties that happen to fall on Friday night.

_____ Rabbi K bans live music at Shabbat afternoon celebrations in the synagogue for weddings or Bar/Bat Mitzvah parties; he permits recordings or tapes of Jewish music if he approves of the selections.

_____ Rabbi L won't permit religious school teachers to use textbooks published by one of the other branches of Judaism.

_____ Rabbi M, along with the other rabbis of his group, adopted an official policy of seeking converts to his own branch of Judaism among (1) Christians who don't belong to any church and (2) Jews who don't belong to any synagogue.

_____ Rabbi N's group of rabbis officially endorsed a frank course on sex and marriage in the upper grades of their religious schools.

_____ Rabbi O organized a *shomrei Shabbat* group in his congregation—"Sabbath-keepers" who observe the Shabbat strictly by worship, study, discussion, song, special Shabbat meals, and fellowship.

Once again, after you fill in your own answers, list beside them the majority answers of the class and compare the two —not to decide "the right answers," but to decide who handled the questions best.

Now that you've argued enough about this, let's take a look at the answers!

Answers to Round Three

Again, the rabbis quoted here are all real persons who actually said or did these things. Here's who said or did what.

· The Reform rabbis were A, E, G, M, N, O.
· The Conservative rabbis were K, L.
· The Orthodox rabbis were B, C, D, F, H, I, J.

This time, you should have had some "don't knows." See if you agree that you could only have guessed about rabbis like D or I as their statements do not give you enough information and could possibly have been made just as well by a Reform or a Conservative rabbi. (If you don't agree, be ready to tell the class your reasons.) Which other rabbis are logically "don't knows"?

You can be pretty sure, on the other hand, about rabbis like B or E. (If you don't agree, why not?) Which others seem logically sure to you?

And how about rabbis H and O—hard to believe, isn't it? Just goes to show you, once more, that you just can't wrap up all Jews into one of three tidy bundles—not until you know much more about them than one or two facts.

ROUND FOUR

Warm-up

Once upon a time, six blind people went to examine an elephant for the first time. One touched the elephant's side and said, "This feels like a wall." Another felt the tusk and said, "This feels like a spear." The third touched the trunk and said, "This feels like a snake." The fourth touched the knee and said, "This feels like a tree." The fifth felt the ears and said, "This feels like a fan." The sixth felt the swinging tail and said, "This feels like a rope."

Question: What's an elephant story doing in a book on Judaism?
Your answer:

_____

_____

_____

_____

Class answer:

_____

_____

_____

_____

R You probably got the point of the warm-up without too much trouble. Terms such as Jew, Judaism, Jewishness; Reform Jews, Conservative Jews, Orthodox Jews—all represent something bigger than anything we can say about them. The elephant isn't just the particular part that you happen to touch.

If you say Jews (or Reform Jews) are this, that, or the other —or that they believe this, don't believe that, do this, don't do that—you're probably forgetting lots of Jews (or Reform Jews) who don't fit your description. You're probably also forgetting lots of non-Jews (or non-Reform Jews) who do fit your description.

Maybe it's better not to say anything about "Jews" or "Reform Jews." If people think you mean all Jews, or all Reform Jews, they can usually trip you up with exceptions. All Jews . . . what? Believe in God? Support Israel? Go to services each week? All Reform Jews . . . what? Pray without hats? Eat non-kosher food? Send their children to a one-day-a-week school?

It won't work—too many exceptions. About all you can safely say if you want no exceptions is: All Jews are Jews. All Reform Jews are Reform Jews. And what good does that do?

Maybe it's safer to use words such as "most, many, some, usually, generally." For instance: Most Jews support Israel. Most Reform Jews don't cover their heads at worship. Many Conservative Jews eat only kosher food. Some Orthodox Jews want changes in Judaism to fit modern needs and conditions. Such statements—if you're very careful about the "most, many, some"—could be valid and hard to challenge.

Does this mean it's absolutely impossible to work out a good solid definition of "Jew" or "Reform Jew" that will work all the time? Or at least most of the time? Let's try a few definitions offered by some people and see what happens. Put on your thinking cap—and don't get frustrated.

Definition No. 1: A Jew is a man (or the wife or child of a man) who either:
- puts on *tefilin* (phylacteries—arm and head straps) every weekday morning, or
- is criticized by somebody for not putting on *tefilin* every weekday morning.

This seems to cover just about every Jew in the world, wouldn't you say? And exclude every non-Jew.

This is the definition of an Orthodox Jew, and it's quite clever. But what's the assumption behind it? That what distinguishes a Jew from a non-Jew—and what makes all Jews alike—is mainly certain observances, ceremonies, rituals, practices. (A Jew either does them or is expected to do them by someone who does them.)

Well, is that the heart, the significance, the basic test of Judaism, Jewishness, the Jewish way of life, the Jewish people? Are practices, as important as they are, the only thing, or the chief thing, that distinguishes a "good" Jew from a "bad" Jew—or a Jew from a non-Jew? Do you agree that there must be more—much more—to it than that?

Let's play around a little with this definition.
Fill in the blanks, here, for yourself:
- A Jew either believes that (or in)_____, or is criticized by others for not believing that (or in) _____. (Careful, now! Did your fill-ins exclude non-Jews?)
- A Jew either acts (in such and such a way)_____,

or is criticized by others for not acting (in such and
such a way)_____.

Try some other verbs in this "equation": A Jew either knows
. . . wants . . . feels . . . tries . . ., or is criticized by others
for not . . . .

_____

_____

Now try it for a particular group of Jews:

· A Reform Jew either_____, or is criticized for
not_____.
· A Conservative Jew either_____, or is criticized for not_____.
· An Orthodox Jew either_____, or is criticized
for not_____.

Finally, let's try to put everything together and say:

A Jew (or a Reform Jew) either observes certain ceremonies . . . believes certain ideas . . . acts in certain ways
. . ., or is criticized by others for not practicing . . . not
believing . . . not acting. . . .

Write below in full detail your own personal definition
or one agreed on by the class.

_____

_____

Does that do it? Does this definition satisfy you? Do you feel
that now you can recognize and define a Jew (or Reform
Jew) accurately and always?

Don't answer yet—we have some more definition games
for you!

Definition No. 2: Centuries past, in the Middle Ages, some
Jews sent the following question to a famous rabbi and
scholar in Spain:

> We have in our town several Jews from a distant country,
> who have been living with us for some time as full-fledged
> Jews. They carry out all religious observances, but they do
> not know the Hebrew names of their fathers. How should
> they be named in our official documents?

The sage—his name was Solomon ibn Adret—could read between the lines as well as anybody else. Do you see what was really bothering them enough to make them send a letter all the way to Spain? Why didn't they just give those people Hebrew names? I think you'll enjoy Rabbi Solomon's rather sharp answer:

> From the tone of your questions . . . you doubt whether
> they are really Jews. . . . If they claim to be Jews, no one
> has the right to investigate their past record, and they are
> to be accepted as full-fledged Jews just as we accept Jews
> of the most distinguished birth. No one has the right to say
> to a Jew "prove that you are a Jew. . . ."

Rabbi Solomon was a great and wise man and a very learned Jew—but don't let that intimidate you. Was he right or wrong? Or was he right in this particular case—in a time when Jews lived almost entirely by themselves and were often persecuted, massacred, exiled—but not necessarily right in general for today? At that time, people who insisted they were Jews were either right or crazy, as they had little to gain and a lot to lose. Today, they have very little to lose.

Anyway, what we're after is Rabbi Solomon ibn Adret's definition of a Jew. Apparently, it goes like this:

> A Jew is anyone who says "I am a Jew" and who actually
> participates in Jewish activities with other Jews.

Again, a simple, all-inclusive definition, quite easy to use. Are Mr. and Mrs. Dalet Jews? Ask them. They are if they say yes; they are not if they say no. Are they "good" Jews? Ask them: yes, if they participate in Jewish activities with other Jews; no, if they don't.

The US census used to agree with Rabbi Solomon ibn Adret—it counted up Jews, Protestants, Catholics, and so on simply by asking people their religion and accepting their answers. But just because the US census agreed does that mean that definition-by-claim always works?

Not in Israel, for one thing. There, some people are always claiming to be Jews (we'll come back to this later) and at times even going to court to convince the Orthodox rabbis and the government. Neither of them takes your word for it —you have to prove it and convince a rabbi or a government official or a judge or the Supreme Court of Israel that your proof is sound.

Another way to test the definition is to turn it around. Suppose people say they are not Jews. They say they never were Jews, have never had anything whatever to do with Jews or Jewish things. Would Rabbi Solomon ibn Adret have accepted this claim simply because the people said so? Would you?

Any Jews can say they are, any non-Jews can say they are, for any reason at all. Isn't something more required than just a person's saying so?

More to come—so don't answer yet.

Definition No. 3: A leading Reform thinker defines a Reform Jew and Reform Judaism this way:

> Reform Judaism includes anything and everything that any Reform Jew does, says, thinks, believes. A Reform Jew is one who is a member of an organized "official" Reform group—a Reform temple, for instance. A Reform group is one that is officially a member of, or belongs to, a national Reform organization—for instance, the Union of American Hebrew Congregations.

One good thing about this definition—it makes it easy to distinguish Reform, Conservative, and Orthodox Jews. The following diagram divides up American Jews according to synagogue membership.

Out of about 6 million Jews in the United States, a million or so belong to Reform synagogues, another million or so to Conservative, and still another million to Orthodox. (Nice, convenient arrangement, isn't it? I wonder how that happened?) Three million don't belong to any congregation but call themselves "Jewish."

There you are! To find out what kind of Jews people are, ask them which million they belong to. If it's one of the first three, you know. If it's one of the last three, you don't know.

This is pretty much like Definition No. 2 (Jews are people who say they're Jews) but it adds *proof-by-membership* in an "official" Jewish organization.

Definition No. 3 runs into trouble the minute you raise some obvious questions about:

· Jews who belong to two or even three different types of synagogues;
· synagogues that call themselves Reform (or Conservative or Orthodox) but are not members of an official national body;
· people who quit their synagogue;
· synagogues that quit the national organization and then rejoin a year later—what they were during that year;
· a Reform member who acts, thinks, talks, believes exactly like most Conservative Jews, or a Conservative member who acts, thinks, talks, believes exactly

like most Reform Jews—what are they, Reform or
Conservative?

If *definition-by-observance* (a Jew does or does not put on
tefilin) and *definition-by-claim* (Jews are those who say
they're Jews) aren't enough, why should *definition-by-mem-
bership* be enough? And what do you think of the idea that
Reform Judaism includes whatever Reform Jews do, think,
and so on? No requirements, no standards, no obligations?
No good or bad, no more or less, no strong or weak, because
anything goes as long as you "belong" to an "official" organization.

It begins to look as if "instant answers" to the question
of defining Jew or Reform, and so on, are just not going to
be enough. You can't just feel the elephant's tail or tusk and
say what that animal is.

You can't look at the iceberg tip above the water and
believe you're seeing the whole iceberg. You can't just say,
"A Jew is . . ." and finish up the sentence, and then sit back
and look at it feeling satisfied that the mystery is all cleared
up and the problem is solved.

But wait—there's one more definition, very popular,
very old, "tried-and-true" that we could work on.

Definition No. 4: This is the standard, traditional Orthodox
definition that goes back centuries, far back to the ancient
past:

> A Jew is anyone born of a Jewish mother, or anyone born
> of a non-Jewish mother if he or she formally converts to
> Judaism.

That's clear enough. Jewish-born (or converted) Jews stay
Jews forever, regardless of what they do or don't do, regardless of what they claim or deny, regardless of what they join
or refuse to join. Proof is required, and proof is by birth or

conversion. (Incidentally, to all Jews, and by all definitions of Jew, converts to Judaism are the equals of born Jews—and must not be made to feel inferior. This means of course that, if a woman converts to Judaism prior to having children, her children must not be looked down upon. They are automatically Jews.)

This "instant answer" has worked well for many centuries, but it doesn't work so well nowadays. It's a different world we live in today, and sometimes a tried-and-true solution to a problem isn't quite as effective as it used to be. That doesn't mean that every tradition doesn't fit modern life—some do and some don't, some fit partly but not completely and need a little "stretching." (Iceberg and elephant again?)

The test of Definition No. 4 (birth or conversion) comes from the growing number of people who have been brought up as Jews since birth, but whose mothers were not Jewish and never converted to Judaism. A Christian woman marries a Jew in Poland and goes with him to Israel where they have a baby. The mother never converts to Judaism, but the child grows up Jewish in every way—speaks Hebrew, keeps Jewish observances, lives and works entirely with Jews and for Jews, is drafted into the army, fights, is wounded for the Jewish state. The child feels Jewish, is treated as Jewish by everyone, and wants to marry "another" Jew.

In Israeli law Jewish marriage is performed only by Orthodox rabbis who "check out" all couples coming to them according to Orthodox Jewish law and tradition. The young man I've been telling you about (this is an actual case) found that, because his mother wasn't a Jew, he wasn't either and couldn't marry a Jewish girl. (If he had died in that war, his family would have found that he couldn't have been buried in a Jewish cemetery!) In such a case, the couple has to go through formal conversion or leave the country, get married somewhere else where it is legal, and then return home.

In our own country, similar situations do come up and not all rabbis, even those of the same branch of Judaism, agree on how to handle it.

> A child is born into a mixed marriage where the mother is not Jewish and has never converted to Judaism. That child is brought up openly and publicly as a Jew. Is that child a Jew or not? Specifically, should a rabbi perform a Jewish wedding ceremony in this case?

Orthodox and Conservative rabbis and many Reform rabbis say no, not until the non-Jewish partner formally and officially converts to Judaism. Some Reform and Conservative rabbis do not raise any questions about it. If a couple and their parents say they are Jewish, these rabbis assume that they are and agree to perform the marriage (Definition No. 2.)

Reconstructionism, the newest branch of Judaism, took action on this point. (The Reconstructionist movement tries to "reconstruct" Jewish life in a way different from that of the Reform, Conservative, or Orthodox Jews; and they have introduced several innovations adopted by Reform and Conservative Jews.) Recently, the Reconstructionists officially and publicly changed the traditional definition of a Jew, accepting as Jewish any person with at least one Jewish parent, provided that person had been brought up as a Jew.

The Reconstructionist announcement rocked Orthodox Jewry which threatened to excommunicate all Reconstructionist Jews. The Orthodox insisted that the Reconstructionist definition will cause heartaches and heartbreaks when people who think they are Jews find out they really aren't. They will have to convert to Judaism before a rabbi will perform their marriage ceremony. The Reconstructionists answered that the heartaches and heartbreaks are caused by the Orthodox definition.

Defining a Jew begins to look like more than "a game," doesn't it? Depending on whether you live in America or Israel, depending on which Jewish branch you belong to, you may find that your Bar/Bat Mitzvah, marriage, divorce, and even burial may depend on who is defining a Jew—and how.

And now—let's try to work out some definitions of our own.

How would you determine the Jewish population of your community? Would you:

_____ take a census and add up those who say they are Jewish?

_____ count up all the members of synagogues?

_____ count up all synagogue members and members of other Jewish organizations?

_____ compare the number of absentees from public school on Jewish holidays and the average attendance on other days and use the difference to figure out how many Jewish families there are?

_____ make a list of Jewish beliefs and practices and then count up everybody who fits that list?

Add below some ideas of your own.

_____

_____

_____

After you've worked out your own answers, find out how your Jewish community leaders actually determine the Jewish population. Try your local Jewish federation, bureau of Jewish education, synagogue organization, rabbis' organization; consult books and articles on Jewish population studies.

You've been asked to draw up a list of Jewish beliefs and practices mentioned in the previous problem. Look at the list below and check off those you would include in such a list.

A Jew:

_____ prays in a synagogue;

_____ observes certain Jewish holidays;

_____ contributes to Jewish organizations;

_____ belongs to a Jewish organization of some kind;

_____ feels personally identified with events of Jewish history;

_____ has a special feeling about the State of Israel;

_____ has a special feeling about certain Jewish symbols;

_____ has a special feeling about certain Jewish foods;

_____ has a special feeling about other Jews.

You can, of course, add some ideas of your own.

_____

_____

_____

Now, go back over the list and add a second check every time the item only fits a Jew and never fits a non-Jew. (Can a non-Jew pray in a synagogue, for instance?) Maybe you'd like to change the wording of some of these items, cross out others, or decide it's impossible to draw up such a list in the first place.

Check, double-check, triple-check, add, reword, cross out—
or give up—on this one:

The term "Jew" refers to:

_____a citizen of ancient Judea;

_____a citizen of modern Israel;

_____a descendant of a people to whom God once revealed
the Torah;

_____a descendant of a people who once made a covenant
with God;

_____a nation;

_____a race;

_____a religion;

_____a people;

_____a culture.

And now some of your own interpretations:

_____

_____

_____

_____

If you're not too worn out by all this, look up "Jew" in
several dictionaries of various sizes (including the un-
abridged) and copy out some of their definitions here.

_____

_____

_____

_____

_____

How do they measure up?

_____

_____

_____

_____

_____

The following actually happened. After your class takes its action, I'll tell you how it turned out.

You and your classmates are delegates to the Illinois Conference of Jewish Organizations. An application for membership in the conference comes in from the Chicago chapter of the American Council for Judaism (ACJ). Discuss this application, then vote on whether the conference should accept or reject the ACJ as a member.

Here is some background for your discussion and decision:

The American Council for Judaism is an organization of Jews who claim to be neither pro-Israel nor anti-Israel, but anti-Zionist. The politics of the State of Israel, they say, is not a part of the Jewish religion. Judaism, for them, is purely religious and has nothing to do with politics, international affairs, or a Jewish nation.

These Jews accuse Zionists, here and in Israel, of trying to use American Jews to promote the political and national interests of the State of Israel. They even go so far, sometimes, as to question the patriotism of American Jews who actively support Israel. They charge that Zionists neglect American problems such as civil rights and poverty, concentrating practically all their efforts and money on Israel's needs and problems.

The ACJ has a small membership of mostly Reform Jews. It has been vigorously denounced by all other Jewish groups, including Reform, Conservative, and Orthodox Jewry. It supports its own synagogues and religious schools and prepares its own textbooks and teaching aids.

The council insists that, though it disagrees about the State of Israel with Zionist Jews, it is a Jewish organization in all respects and is entitled to representation in a general association of Jewish organizations.

Their opponents insist that they speak only for a few misguided Jews who are so afraid of being called "un-American" that they do great harm both to Israel and to American Jews. The Chicago chapter of the ACJ, for example, did nothing to help Israel during the terrible crisis of the Six Day War of June, 1967—and they were practically the only Jews in the world who did nothing. Their explanation for not taking action was: "Our office was closed for the summer." The national office, though, was not closed for the summer —it sent money to the Arab refugees.

Finally, charge their opponents, their officers are the only Jews that certain Arab governments ever permitted to travel in their countries.

Here's some additional information that may be of use to you: A year later some of the ACJ's top leaders resigned or were discharged, with no clear reasons ever given publicly. One official who left accused the others of helping Arab representatives at the United Nations write their speeches and of refusing to aid persecuted Jews in Arab countries, even though they had great personal influence there.

Think it over. Remember, you're not deciding whether the American Council for Judaism is right or wrong—but whether or not the Illinois Conference of Jewish Organizations should accept the Chicago chapter of the ACJ as a member. Does every Jewish organization have to agree with every other one? Is the ACJ a Jewish organization, even though it is an anti-Israel minority among American Jews? Are its members harmful, dangerous, "traitors" to the Jewish cause? Will it help or hurt the rest of us to take them in? Will it help or hurt them?

Thrash it all out, take your vote, and record it here:

_____

_____

On the question of accepting the Chicago chapter of the American Council for Judaism as a member of the Illinois Conference of Jewish Organizations, we have voted (if you have a tie vote, let your teacher decide):

_____unanimously;

_____by a majority of_____to_____;

_____to accept their application because_____

_____;

_____to reject their application because_____

_____;

_____to table (postpone) our decision because _____

_____;

_____to accept their application, only if_____

_____ .

Now, read on to find out what really happened!

The Illinois conference voted no and rejected the application.

You can wind up this discussion by preparing a class letter to the Illinois Conference of Jewish Organizations (see your librarian for the address), approving their decision and saying why or disapproving their decision and saying why.

You can also wind up this section—and get ready for the next one—by writing to the following organizations, asking for information about their activities. When their pamphlets and magazines arrive, you can arrange them for a table or bulletin board display and discuss any questions they raise in your mind.

American Jewish Committee
165 E. 56 St., New York, NY 10022.

American Jewish Congress
15 E. 84 St., New York, NY 10028.

American Jewish Joint Distribution Committee
60 E. 42 St., New York, NY 10036.

American ORT Federation
817 Broadway, New York, NY 10003.

B'nai B'rith
823 UN Plaza, New York, NY 10017.

Canadian Jewish Congress
1590 Ave. Docteur Penfield, Montreal, PQ, H3G 1C5,
Can.

Council of Jewish Federations and Welfare Funds
575 Lexington Ave., New York, NY 10022.

Jewish Community Relations Council
111 W. 40 St., New York, NY 10018.

Jewish National Fund
42 E. 69 St., New York, NY 10021.

Union of American Hebrew Congregations
838 Fifth Ave., New York, NY 10021.

Union of Orthodox Jewish Congregations
45 W. 36 St., New York, NY 10018.

United Synagogue of America
155 Fifth Ave., New York, NY 10012.

Question: Should you also include the American Council for Judaism? If you don't include them, are you rejecting them as Jews? If you do include them, are you accepting them— or just getting more information to help you make up your mind?

In case you want it, here's the address:

American Council for Judaism
307 Fifth Ave., New York, NY 10016.

How do you feel now? Confused? Unhappy? More mixed up than ever? Or have you realized we're tackling a really tough problem that has no "instant answers"?

We told you at the very beginning that this unit aimed to confuse you, show you how hard a nut we have to crack!

But cheer up—the next unit tries to explore some answers.

UNIT II

Some Real Differences?
Come Let's Understand
One Another and Why
We Differ

First, look up and fill in the following information (insert inside parentheses whether Reform, Conservative, or Orthodox).

	Nearest synagogue of your own branch of Judaism ( )	Nearest synagogue of (two) other branches ( ) ( )
Name		
Address		
Phone		
Rabbi		
Cantor		
President		
Principal		
Committee chairperson		
Youth leader		
Any other official		

Next, phone, write, or visit a leader in all three congregations to ask the following questions. Do it yourself or get classmates to divide up the work with you or help you with it. Tape record or make notes of the answers.

1. Have all three congregations, or any two of them, ever engaged in some joint effort or project in the past? If so, what? If now engaged in such a project, what? If considering or planning one, what?

2. Whatever the answers, why or why not? If the answer to any of the above is yes, how well did the joint project succeed, or how badly did it fail, and why?

3. What kinds of joint projects do congregations seem to cooperate and succeed in (educational, religious, camping, parent or teacher education, fundraising, community improvement, etc.)? What kinds do they generally not cooperate or not succeed very well in, when they do?

4. What sorts of reasons and motives do congregations have for cooperating in joint projects? For not doing so?

Finally, your report. Consult your teacher on whether it is to be oral or written and what form it should take. Do not spend too much time on the actual answers you get—just give them briefly. Rather, emphasize your own conclusions about questions 3 and 4 above.

ROUND ONE

Warm-up

Some basic questions for you. Talk them over first—in class, at home, with your rabbi, principal, other adults. Then write your answers:

1. What is the single most important way that Reform, Conservative, and Orthodox Jews differ from one another?

    _____
    _____
    _____
    _____

2. What are two other important differences? (Give more than two if you like.)

    a. _____
    _____
    b. _____
    _____
    c. _____

3. What is the single most important way that they are all alike?

    _____
    _____
    _____
    _____

4. What are two other important similarities? (More if you like.)

    a. _____
    _____

b. _____

_____

c. _____

_____

After class discussion, or tally of answers, write down the class majority answer:

1. _____

_____

_____

_____

2. a. _____

_____

b. _____

_____

c. _____

_____

3. _____

_____

_____

_____

4. a. _____

_____

b. _____

_____

c. _____

_____

· Congregations sometimes switch from Conservative to Reform and vice versa.

- In quite a few Reform religious schools there are teachers who are Conservative Jews, in some cases even Orthodox Jews; in at least one case, a Reform religious school faculty has included an Orthodox rabbi.
- Some Jews belong to two different kinds of synagogues.
- Reform textbooks are often used in Conservative schools and vice versa; the Reform movement and the Conservative movement have co-published classroom materials, conducted joint family programs in camps, and co-sponsored educational conferences.
- Many Reform rabbis are personally as "observant" as Conservative and even Orthodox rabbis.

How come? Which of the following do you think might be part of the explanation? Check off your answers.

_____ There isn't really much difference between Reform and Conservative.

_____ People don't really understand the difference.

_____ People are tolerant and broad-minded.

_____ People aren't really sincere.

_____ Nothing important prevents Reform and Conservative from combining into one group.

_____ Other explanation: _____

_____

_____

_____

The following situations actually occurred. After you've decided what you would do, we'll tell you what really happened.

Situation A: In a large eastern city, a group of young adults started a Conservative congregation. But, after a time, most of them felt uncomfortable with the Conservative approach and began to consider becoming an Orthodox congregation. A delegation of congregants found out more about Orthodox Judaism and reported back to the congregation which made the final decision.

Situation B: The leadership and many members of a Reform temple on the West Coast found themselves doubting whether they were really Reform Jews or would feel more at home if they affiliated with the Conservative movement. A special committee studied both movements for a year and reached a decision which the congregation accepted.

Choose Situation A or B (or both). In a simulation (fancy name for "let's pretend") you and some classmates have the responsibility of advising the congregation which way to go.

1. Where would you go, whom could you talk to or write for help, information, advice?

    _____

    _____

    _____

    _____

2. List some books and magazines your committee might read and discuss to help you reach a decision.

    _____

    _____

    _____

    _____

3. Have your committee decide what to recommend and why.

_____
_____
_____
_____

4. Take a class vote for or against your committee's recommendation. We have voted:
   _____unanimously;
   _____by a majority of_____to_____;
   _____to accept the committee's recommendation;
   _____to reject the committee's recommendation.

5. Fill in this record of your simulation:
   We started out as a_____congregation affiliated with_____.
   Many of us wanted to change to a(n)_____congregation affiliated with_____.
   After studying and discussing the matter, we decided to:
   _____remain as we are, a_____congregation affiliated with_____;
   _____change to a(n)_____congregation affiliated with_____;
   _____table the problem until we have studied and discussed it some more.

6. Think about your simulation:
   a. What problems came up that bothered you?

   _____
   _____
   _____
   _____

   b. What were your reasons for your decisions?

   _____
   _____
   _____
   _____

c. What things of special interest did you learn about the Reform, Conservative, or Orthodox movements?

_____

_____

_____

_____

Now, read on to find out what really happened!

In Situation A, the Conservative synagogue, which had been started with the help of the United Synagogue of America (the national organization of Conservative synagogues), sent a delegation to Yeshiva University in New York City to learn about Orthodox practices. The delegates found that Orthodox Judaism appealed to them more than Conservative Judaism because they enjoyed stricter ritual observance. Yeshiva University gave them funds and suggested a talented young Orthodox rabbi as their spiritual leader. Under his direction, they changed their synagogue into an Orthodox congregation and are quite pleased about it.

In Situation B, the committee of the Reform congregation met regularly for a year. They not only read and discussed numerous books and magazines but invited lay leaders, rabbis, and educators of both movements to meet with them and answer their questions. Their final decision was to remain in the Reform movement and continue to affiliate with the Union of American Hebrew Congregations (the national organization of Reform synagogues).

A town has only two synagogues. One is Reform, the other Conservative. Parents who feel their children's Jewish education lacks an understanding and appreciation of Orthodox Judaism have asked the two religious school boards to hold a joint meeting to discuss the problem and plan a joint project to teach all the children about Orthodox Judaism.

What happens? Do both religious school boards agree to meet or does one refuse—and, if so, why? And what happens then?

In planning for such a meeting, what are the arguments for and against the parents' request?

_____

_____

_____

If the decision is made to act, what various alternatives would you suggest to solve the problem?

_____

_____

_____

Which alternative do you think would be the best to most school board members?

_____

_____

Your job: Work up a news report based on your answers to these questions. Classmates with other answers could work up their own news reports and the class could decide which "scenario" it prefers.

Or: With classmates, act out the meeting, first according to your answers, then according to the opposite answers, or different answers. The class decides which one it prefers.

How do you feel now?

_____ I think it's sometimes very hard to tell the difference between Reform, Conservative, and Orthodox, and you have to be rather careful about it.

_____ I'm all mixed up.

_____ I still feel sure I can tell Reform, Conservative, and Orthodox Jews apart, even if I can't put it into words.

ROUND TWO

Hats On! Hats Off! The Great Yarmulke Debate

Recently, for a Bar Mitzvah ceremony in a Reform temple, the boy's grandfather asked if he could wear a *kipah* (skullcap) and a *talit* (prayer shawl).

If you were the rabbi, what would you have said?

_____ Yes.

_____ No.

What sort of rule would you make about it—and why?

_____

_____

A Reform temple should:

· forbid *kipot* and *taliyot* because _____

_____

· permit anyone wishing to wear them to do so because

_____

_____

· require everyone to do so because _____

In the case above, the synagogue board said no. And, when the boy's parents went to the rabbi, he supported his officers.

"Why," he asked, "should anyone insist on wearing a *kipah* or a *talit?* They have no ethical meaning. Not wearing them won't hurt anyone's ethics, morals, or Jewishness."

If it were your son's Bar Mitzvah, or your daughter's Bat Mitzvah, would you have:

_____ forced the temple's ruling on your parent, the grandfather?

_____ accepted it even if your parent, the grandfather, refused to come?

_____ changed over to another synagogue?

How important is wearing a *kipah* or a *talit?* _____

How important is it if wearing a *kipah* or a *talit* is vitally important to someone else? _____

This particular   family changed over to another synagogue. Were they right?_____
The Reform rabbi was quite serious when he claimed that Reform Judaism had a "secret weapon" which, if used, would turn most Conservative Jews into Reform Jews overnight. (The secret weapon: wearing a *kipah.*) If Reform Jews, this rabbi says, adopt the custom of wearing a *kipah,* Conservative Jews will join Reform temples in droves.

> Maybe it's that important a custom, that important an element of Judaism? Maybe that's the only thing that keeps Reform and Conservatives apart? And maybe it works the other way, too? Maybe Conservative Jews, just by giving up the *kipah,* could have Reform Jews turning Conservative in droves?

Let's explore this controversial topic and decide later if it's a major or a minor issue. We'll begin by going back into history—partly to remind you, as the Bible says, that "there's nothing new under the sun" (Ecclesiastes 1:9) and partly to help you understand "tradition" and how it works. Then we'll return to the present for an analysis of today's view. And only then should you venture to decide how important an issue it is to wear or not to wear a *kipah.*

Example No. 1: Solomon Luria (1510–1573) was a great rabbi and scholar in Poland. He once received this question from another rabbi:

> May someone who has a headache eat and say the blessings bareheaded?

The idea was, of course, that the weight of a hat or head covering might make a headache more painful. Was it therefore all right to perform a religious act bareheaded, as a matter of health and comfort?

Now read Luria's answer carefully—remember, this was four hundred years ago!

> I know of no law against saying the blessings with an uncovered head. . . . It is quite clear from *Midrash Rabbah* that we may proclaim the *Shema* with a bare head. The *Midrash Rabbah* purposely contrasts God with a human king, to indicate that it is even more dignified to read the *Shema* with a bare head, as that shows greater reverence than to read it with covered head. As Judaism prefers dignity and simplicity in its services, the Jews were excused from worshiping God in the pompous, pretentious manner which other peoples used to honor their kings.
>
> Yet, I cannot permit myself to say the *Shema* bareheaded, because the people have come to accept this as prohibited. I am surprised, however, that the authorities have prohibited uncovering the head even when one is not praying. . . .
>
> Nevertheless, a scholar should keep his head covered; otherwise, people will consider him light-minded and frivolous as if he had actually violated Jewish law. . . .

Of course, there were no Reform, Conservative, or Orthodox branches in the sixteenth century—everybody was "orthodox."

How would you describe Solomon Luria's ideas in today's language?

_____Reform?

_____Conservative?

_____Orthodox?

Luria was a fascinating character, with sharp mind and tongue and fearless about attacking even the rich and powerful for ethical violations; yet he was a practical man with lots of common sense. Notice how he distinguishes between:

- the actual facts about custom;
- the mistaken notion most people had about the custom;
- the duty of a respected rabbi to go along with the people's notion, even though wrong.

Write down what you think made him go along with the people's notion.

_____

_____

_____

_____

Opinion No. 1: Head covering was an ancient custom among eastern peoples for women to cover their hair and sometimes even their faces. Men usually did not do this indoors. It became the custom in Europe in the Middle Ages for men to uncover their heads as a sign of respect before a king or a nobleman during worship. Jewish men, likewise, in Europe, during the Middle Ages, usually did not cover their heads, even in synagogue.

Opinion No. 2: In Babylonia, some rabbis and scholars began to cover their heads as a special sign of respect and reverence before God. Other Jews adopted the custom, and it gradually spread to all other European countries. By Luria's time, Jews everywhere believed it was wrong to pray, or do anything else, without a head covering.

Opinion No. 3: The Talmud (compiled about the year 500 C.E.) only mildly criticizes bareheadedness as being discourteous to God, implying that a covered head is more respectful and may help give you a feeling of worship and reverence. (The *Shulchan Aruch*—a Jewish rulebook, published in 1555 and still the official code of Jewish law for Orthodox Jews—declares that a man may not walk four cubits—a cubit is equal to 18 inches—bareheaded. In other words, an Orthodox Jew is never permitted to go without head covering.)

Opinion No. 4: Less than two hundred years ago, in Lithuania, the greatest Jewish scholar of the time, Elijah of Vilna, answered the same question the same way as Solomon Luria did: one may pray without head covering but it is good manners to cover the head.

So—head-covering is not really an ancient Jewish "law." It developed gradually, over the centuries. You can also see that Jews had different customs in different countries and different times!

Example No. 2: A Yiddish story, *The Three Gifts,* by the great writer, I. L. Peretz, tells of a soul that was sent back from heaven to earth to find the three most precious gifts in the universe. One gift the soul brought back was a cap from the head of an old Jew who was beaten to death by hoodlums. He could have gotten away, but as his *kipah* fell he turned back to get it and cover his head; and so he died under the blows.

Opinion No. 1: Very observant Orthodox Jews wear a head-covering all the time. Some Orthodox and Conservative Jews wear a *kipah* only while praying. Reform Jews may or may not wear a *kipah.* Many do as a matter of individual choice and will, of course, wear one in a Conservative or Orthodox synagogue or ceremony.

You're probably wondering how—after the Talmud

and the *Shulchan Aruch,* Solomon Luria and Elijah of Vilna
—the *kipah* has come to be so important a symbol for Conservative and Orthodox Jews. One possible answer: It became so in defensive reaction against the early "reformers"
and the changes they made in many accepted practices.
The *kipah* came to symbolize the entire Orthodox way of
life in contrast with the new "Reform" ideas about Jewish
life.

Opinion No. 2: Some Jews today in our own country
wear a *kipah* not so much because they are Orthodox, or
because they think it is an ancient custom or a commandment of God, but as a public symbol that they are Jewish and
will remain Jewish no matter what.

During the freedom marches for civil rights in the six-
ties, many rabbis marched wearing *kipot,* and black leaders
took it up as a symbol and put *kipot* on their own heads.

> How important is the wearing of a
> *kipah?*

Complete the following statements.

From a Reform Jew: I'm completely opposed to wearing a *kipah* at any time, because _____

_____

_____

From another Reform Jew: I don't see any need to
wear a *kipah,* but I'd wear it if I'm with
Conservative or Orthodox Jews who are
wearing it, and I'd allow others in my temple
to wear it if they wanted to. My reasons are

_____

_____

_____

From both a Conservative and an Orthodox Jew: I
wear a *kipah* and expect others to wear it
when I do, because _____

_____

_____

Test out your answers by asking a few people from each
branch of Judaism how they feel about the *kipah* debate, and
why. Start with your own parents, if you wish. Summarize
the answers you get and report below how they compare
with yours.

_____

_____

_____

_____

_____

1. In a letter to the editor of a Jewish newspaper, a reader
objected to photos showing two bareheaded professors
identified as "talmud teachers" at a Jewish college. The
reader said this showed "disrespect for tradition" and
accused the two professors of "playing scholars."

    Write a letter in reply, have your classmates and
your teacher go over it, and send it to your temple
bulletin.

2. What is your own congregation's policy concerning the
kipah?

    _____permitted;

    _____forbidden;

    _____encouraged;

    _____discouraged.

3. Take a *"kipah* poll" during at least two different services in your synagogue.

How many worshipers present?_____

How many wearing *kipot?*_____

Fraction or percentages?_____

How many men and boys wearing *kipot?*_____

How many women and girls?_____

Fractions and percentages?_____

Is there a difference in percentages between the males and females who wear *kipot?*_____

If the answer is yes, give reason for that.

_____

_____

_____

Write a letter to your rabbi about your findings, conclusions, and opinions—after, of course, first discussing them with your classmates and your teacher.

1. Is it at all possible that opinions on the *kipah,* pro and con, will ever change?_____

Why? _____

_____

2. If opinion ever does change, which is more likely to happen—for Conservatives to give up the *kipah,* or for Reform Jews to adopt it? _____

_____

_____

Why? _____

_____

_____

3. Whichever way, would the change really make much difference? Would a great many Reform or Conservative Jews join the other type of synagogue just because of a change in the rule or custom of head-covering? Are there deeper, more important differences that would keep Reform and Conservative Jews separate, even if there were no *kipah* problem? _____
   _____
   _____
   _____

ROUND THREE
ABOUT VARIOUS THINGS

1. *About Beards*

Not too long ago, all Orthodox rabbis wore beards, on the basis of a biblical verse (Leviticus 21:5—look it up!). In fact, many Jews then wouldn't believe a man was a rabbi unless he wore a beard. (There were no women rabbis.)

Today, things have changed. We have women rabbis and clean-shaven Orthodox rabbis. (They use a special cream that washes away their beard, so they are not violating the biblical ban on shaving or cutting.)

What conclusions do you draw from this change?

_____

_____

_____

_____

_____

_____

2. *About the Talit and Tefilin*

Wearing a *talit* is based on Numbers 15:37–41. (Look it up!) Orthodox Jews and many Conservatives wear it at weekday morning worship services as well as during Shabbat and holiday services. In Reform worship, many rabbis wear a *talit;* and some Reform synagogues make *taliyot* available, along with *kipot,* for worshipers who wish to wear them.

Tefilin consist of leather boxes and straps worn on the head and left arm at weekday morning services. The boxes contain four separate portions from the Torah: 13:1–10, 11–16 from Exodus and 6:4–9, 11:13–21 from Deuteronomy.

The straps symbolically represent important religious themes. For the biblical commandment regarding *tefilin*, look up Deuteronomy 6:8 and 11:18.

No special prayer is recited when putting on a *kipah*, but prayers are said when donning *talit* and *tefilin*. The old Union prayer book of 1940 did not contain these prayers. The new Union prayer book of 1975, *Gates of Prayer*, does contain these prayers (on pp. 48–49, under the heading, "For those who wear the *talit*" and "For those who wear *tefilin*").

The *talit* and the *tefilin* have their own interesting stories, their own unusual details symbolizing certain basic Jewish beliefs. Look these up in Jewish encyclopedias and books about Jewish worship in your synagogue library.

Note here anything you find that is of special interest to you.

_____

_____

_____

_____

_____

_____

_____

_____

_____

_____

Talk to your rabbi about your synagogue's practice and the rabbi's personal practice regarding *talit* and *tefilin*.

60

Note here anything you learn that is of special interest to you.

_____

_____

_____

_____

_____

_____

_____

_____

_____

ROUND FOUR

About "G-d"

Orthodox Jews will not write, print, or pronounce the formal names of God—Adonai and Elohim—in daily use. They consider doing so a violation of one of the Ten Commandments. (Look up the Ten Commandments in either Exodus 20:2–14 or Deuteronomy 5:6–18 and write the appropriate commandment here.)

_____

_____

_____

These two formal names appear in the Hebrew of the Bible and the prayer book. But Orthodox Jews use an abbreviation in ordinary printing, writing, and speaking. They use the letter ה or ד to stand for Adonai. For Hebrew numbers, they do not represent 15 by using the letters 10 and 5 (*yod* and *hay*), neither for 16 the letters 10 and 6 (*yod* and *vav*), since these combinations are part of the Hebrew name, Adonai, and would therefore violate the commandment. Instead they use the letters 9 and 6 (*tet* and *vav*) and 9 and 7 *(tet* and *zayin).* In speech, they say *"Adoshem"* and *"Elokenu,"* or just *"Hashem"* (the Name).

This concern about not using God's name in Hebrew has carried over to the English language. So they write or print "G-d" instead of "God" and "L--d" instead of "Lord."

To the Orthodox, the very paper on which you write "God" becomes sacred and holy, like the Torah scrolls, the Bible, and the prayer book. The paper cannot be scribbled on or crushed or thrown away. But they say, using G-d does not affect the paper; it's not holy, and you can do with it whatever you want.

Does our respect for God's name imply that we must use substitutes or abbreviations everywhere but in the Bible and the prayer book? Does typing or writing a hyphen instead of an "o" show greater respect for God? Does the Hebrew language as such have any special "holiness" attached to it? Put down your reactions here:

_____

_____

_____

_____

_____

_____

_____

_____

_____

_____

ROUND FIVE

About Women and Bat Mitzvah

Linda   Sarah   Rachel

Ready for a real puzzler?

Here are three Jewish sisters, raised by Orthodox parents. Each of the three women has opted for a different branch of Judaism.

Linda, the oldest, has maintained her affiliation with her parents' Orthodox shul, Sarah belongs to a Conservative synagogue, while Rachel recently joined a Reform temple. Each of the sisters graduated from college with high academic honors.

Now the puzzle: As teenagers, Linda, Sarah, and Rachel decided they would like to be rabbis. Therefore, after college:

 Linda applied to an Orthodox rabbinical school;

 Sarah applied to the Conservative movement's Jewish Theological Seminary;

Rachel applied to the Reform movement's Hebrew Union College-Jewish Institute of Religion.

Yet, despite the fact that each sister had a superb college record, only one was granted an interview!

Can you guess which one? And why? Write your answer here:

I think_____got the interview, because _____

_____

_____

_____

_____

_____

Now let's see if you were right!

If your answer was Rachel, you are correct! Rachel was the only sister invited for an interview.

> But the real question is "Why?"

Fact No. 1: The Reform movement, through the Hebrew Union College-Jewish Institute of Religion, was the first major Jewish body to ordain a woman as a rabbi.

Fact No. 2: As of 1982, the Reform movement was the only one of the three largest Jewish movements to have ordained women rabbis.

Fact No. 3: By 1982, the Reconstructionists had ordained a number of women, while the Conservative movement was still debating the issue.

And now, for a discussion of Bat Mitzvah, let's go back to:

Linda   *Sarah*   *Rachel*

Over the years, each of the three sisters raised a family. Each had two children, a boy and a girl.

The families joyfully celebrated their sons' Bar Mitzvahs. Then came the Bat Mitzvah dilemma.

Linda (Orthodox) went to her shul to arrange for her daughter's Bat Mitzvah and was told that there was no such ceremony. On the other hand, Sarah (Conservative) and Rachel (Reform) visited their rabbis and were happy to learn that their daughters' Bat Mitzvah ceremonies were to be every bit as rich in traditional material.

> Why the difference?

Fact No. 1: Reform Judaism along with the conservative movement adopted Bat Mitzvah from the Reconstructionists. However, no Orthodox congregation I know of either has an "equal" Bat Mitzvah ceremony or is even discussing having one!

Fact No. 2: Orthodox Judaism views women and their religious role in Judaism far differently from the more liberal denominations, particularly Reform Judaism. For a variety of reasons, Orthodox Judaism holds the following:

· The most important role of women is as homemakers and wives.

- Because of this priority, Orthodox women are not required to perform any of the positive *mitzvot* that must be done at certain set times (i.e., praying three times a day).
- Women cannot be rabbis.
- Women cannot read from the Torah.
- Women cannot sit with men at services.

From its inception, on an official level, Reform declared that women were to be equal to men in all religious matters. Read the following excerpts from official Reform conferences in Europe and America. What do these statements tell you about Reform's stance vis-à-vis the issue of women's equality?

The Rabbinical Conference shall declare the female sex as religiously equal with the male, in its obligations and rights, and pronounce accordingly as halakhic:

1. that women must observe all *mitzvot,* even though they pertain to a certain time, in so far as these *mitzvot* have any strength and vigor at all for our religious consciousness;
2. that the female sex has to fulfil all obligations towards children in the same manner as the male;
3. that neither the husband nor the father has the right to absolve a religiously mature daughter or wife from her vow;
4. that, from now on, the benediction *shelo asani ishah,* which was the basis for the religious prejudice against woman, shall be abolished;
5. that the female sex shall, from earliest youth, be obligated to participate in religious instruction and public worship, and in the latter respect also be counted in a *minyan;*

6. that the religious coming of age for both sexes begins with the age of thirteen. (Report to the Breslau Conference, 1846)

If at all possible, all members of the community shall be involved in participating in the tasks of the community, especially in the area of charity and social welfare. The participation of women in religious and communal life is indispensable. They should receive their equal share in religious duties as well as rights. (Guidelines for a Program of Liberal Judaism, 1912)

The ordination of woman as rabbi is a modern issue due to the evolution in her status in our day. The Central Conference of American Rabbis has repeatedly made pronouncements urging the fullest measure of self-expression for woman as well as the fullest utilization of her gifts in the service of the Most High and gratefully acknowledges the enrichment and enlargement of congregational life which has resulted therefrom.

Whatever may have been the specific legal status of the Jewish woman regarding certain religious functions, her general position in Jewish religious life has ever been an exalted one. She has been the priestess in the home, and our sages have always recognized her as the preserver of Israel. In view of these Jewish teachings and in keeping with the spirit of our age and the traditions of our conference, we declare that woman cannot justly be denied the privilege of ordination. (Central Conference of American Rabbis, 1922)

The Equal Rights Amendment recognized the inherent rights and concomitant responsibilities of women as co-equal with men. If adopted, it would rectify long-standing injustices which have deprived women of education, employment, and financial opportunities equal to men as well as end discriminatory public laws which have contributed to a second-class status for women in American society. (General Assembly of the Union of American Hebrew Congregations, 1973)

1. Based on these excerpts, how would you describe Reform Judaism's position on women?

_____
_____
_____
_____
_____
_____
_____

2. How does the liberal position differ from that of Orthodoxy?

_____
_____
_____
_____
_____
_____
_____

Fact No. 1: When it comes to the rights and privileges of women in Judaism, Reform and Orthodoxy diverge sharply. In Reform, women are accorded official equality in all things Jewish. In Orthodoxy, women are excused or even proscribed from performing certain religious roles on the grounds that their responsibility lies elsewhere.

Fact No. 2: Even though Reform Judaism has a long way to go before women attain in practice the full equality they enjoy in official movement pronouncements, still, there are today women rabbis, cantors, educators, administrators, and temple presidents of Reform congregations. They serve on the boards of trustees of the Union of American Hebrew Congregations and the Hebrew Union College–Jewish Institute of Religion. No other major movement has a similar record of accomplishment. In this instance, at least, Reform is unique.

Several years ago, hundreds of thousands of Jewish women signed a "Petition to Rabbinical Authorities" and sent it to Reform, Conservative, and Orthodox rabbinical associations. The petition requested a "reinterpretation" or "modification" of certain Jewish religious laws that the signers considered unfair to Jewish women. They also requested a world assembly of rabbinic authorities to study the problem and the hardships caused by these laws.

Carry out any of the following actions that interest you:

1. Write to any of the women's organizations listed at the end of this round. Mention the petition and ask for examples of laws they consider unfair to Jewish women as well as for the latest information on the problem.

    In writing to the National Federation of Temple Sisterhoods (Reform) and the Women's League of the United Synagogue (Conservative), also ask what is the official position of the movement on women's rights, duties, and privileges in Jewish life and inquire if there are any women rabbis, cantors, and synagogue presidents in their movement, and if so how many?

2. Write to one of the rabbinical associations listed below. Mention the petition, ask for the latest information on the problem and their official position on women's rights, duties, and privileges in Jewish life and request examples of women rabbis, cantors, and synagogue presidents.

3. Display your replies on a poster or the bulletin board along with a statement of your own on "The Status of Women in the Movement(s)."

4. After consulting your teacher, give the class an oral report.

How much of a problem would the status of women be in discussing a merger of any two of our religious groups?

_____impossible;

_____major;

_____important;

_____minor;

_____little or none.

Explain your answer.

_____

_____

_____

_____

_____

_____

_____

WOMEN'S ORGANIZATIONS

American Jewish Congress Women
15 E. 84 St., New York, NY 10028.

B'nai B'rith Women
823 UN Plaza, New York, NY 10017.

Hadassah
50 W. 58 St., New York, NY 10019.

International Council of Jewish Women
15 E. 26 St., New York, NY 10010.

National Council of Jewish Women
15 E. 26 St., New York, NY 10010.

National Federation of Temple Sisterhoods
Union of American Hebrew Congregations
838 Fifth Ave., New York, NY 10021.

Pioneer Women
200 Madison Ave., New York, NY 10016.

Task Force on Equality of Women in Judaism
New York Federation of Reform Synagogues
838 Fifth Ave., New York, NY 10021.

Union of Orthodox Jewish Congregations of America
(Women's Branch)
45 W. 36, New York, NY 10018.

Women's League for Conservative Judaism
48 E. 74 St., New York, NY 10021.

RABBINICAL ASSOCIATIONS

Central Conference of American Rabbis (Reform)
21 E. 40 St., New York, NY 10016.

Rabbinical Assembly of America (Conservative)
3080 Broadway, New York, NY 10027.

Rabbinical Council of America (Orthodox)
1250 Broadway, New York, NY 10001.

ROUND SIX

About "Jews by Choice"

There are two ways in which one can become a Jew: (a) by birth, (b) through conversion.

Nobody ever questions the "credentials" of a born Jew, even if that individual has little or nothing to do with Judaism. Unfortunately, however, stereotypes and prejudice all too often mar our relationships with Jews who have come to Judaism later in life through conversion.

Here are five statements about Judaism and its position on converts or "Jews by choice." Mark each statement TRUE or FALSE.

_____ 1. Judaism has always discouraged people from converting to Judaism.

_____ 2. Converts know less about Judaism than born Jews.

_____ 3. Unless you were born Jewish, you can never "really" be a Jew.

_____ 4. Reform, Conservative, and Orthodox Jews basically agree on the requirements for conversion.

_____ 5. Unless your mother was a Jew, you are not considered to be a born Jew.

Okay, now let's see how you did.

Answers to Round Six

Statement No. 1: Judaism has always discouraged people from converting to Judaism.
Answer: False.

The first Jew, Abraham, was a convert. The Bible, in fact, refers to his missionary activity on behalf of Judaism thousands of years ago. Indeed, according to some historians, Judaism once had hundreds of missionaries. By the fourth century C.E., Christian and Moslem governments, hoping to eliminate Judaism, ruled that Jews could no longer seek converts. In spite of the fact that violation of these laws was punishable by death, Jews continued to seek and embrace converts until about 1600. It was only then, less than four hundred years ago, that proselytization (another word for seeking converts) was abandoned by the Jewish community, the result of Jews being forced to live in ghettos, of pogroms that killed thousands of innocent Jews, and of new laws declaring that Jewish missionizing was punishable by death.

What do we learn from this?

Fact No. 1: Jewish opposition to conversion is a relatively recent development in Jewish history.

Fact No. 2: Looking at the total scope of Jewish history, Judaism has encouraged missionary activity.

A careful reading of rabbinic literature (such as the Talmud) indicates an overwhelmingly positive attitude toward those who choose Judaism as their faith. See if you can find five concrete references to converts in midrashic or talmudic literature. Ask your rabbi, educator, or teacher to help you.

Summarize the accounts here.

1. _____

_____
_____
_____

2. _____

_____

_____

_____

3. _____

_____

_____

_____

4. _____

_____

_____

_____

5. _____

_____

_____

_____

Here's some information that may be of use to you: In December of 1978, responding to the rising rate of inter-marriage and the hunger for spirituality of millions of Americans, Rabbi Alexander M. Schindler, president of the Union of American Hebrew Congregations, proposed a program of "Outreach" that had the following three major aims:

1. To welcome converts and involve them in Judaism, recognizing that those who choose Judaism are as authentic in their Jewish identity as those who are born Jewish.
2. To develop programs for mixed married couples that make the congregation, the rabbi, and Judaism itself more open to them and their families.
3. To carry the message of Judaism to any and all who wish to examine or embrace it. Judaism is not an exclusive club of born Jews; it is a universal faith with an ancient tradition which has deep significance for many people today.

Reaction to Rabbi Schindler's address was swift. Many Orthodox leaders launched a bitter attack on him and the Outreach concept. Liberal Jews generally accepted the idea of Outreach, but some expressed reservations about the missionary activity implied in part three of the program.

I think the three major emphases of the Outreach program are good ideas (or bad ideas) because (discuss each one separately):

1. _____
_____
_____

2. _____
_____
_____

3. _____
_____
_____

Why do you think the Orthodox Jewish community expressed such violent opposition to Outreach?

_____
_____
_____

Let's go on to Statement No. 2 and see if, together, we can discover some answers.

Statement No. 2: Converts know less about Judaism than born Jews.
Answer: Not necessarily true.

The great majority of born Jews unfortunately do not continue their Jewish education beyond Bar/Bat Mitzvah or Confirmation. Accordingly, though attending Jewish schools for seven to ten years, they rarely if ever grapple with the most profound and sophisticated Jewish ideas. And, by adulthood, much factual learning acquired as children has been forgotten.

The great majority of those who convert to Judaism, however, do so as adults, studying privately with a rabbi or attending a special course. Because these individuals have come to Judaism in their later years, their study of Judaism, though relatively brief, often embraces many of the great ideas of Judaism on a sophisticated level.

What do we learn from this?

Fact No. 1: While we cannot claim absolute accuracy, it appears that the average "Jew by choice" may study at least as many facts about Judaism as the average "Jew by birth" with a Bar/Bat Mitzvah level education.

Fact No. 2: Those who convert to Judaism seem to be the ones of the few groups of Jewish adults who study the full panorama of Jewish thought, ritual, and history on a sophisticated level.

Fact No. 3: Contrary to the popular stereotype, it may be that those who convert to Judaism know as much or more about Judaism than the average "Jew by birth."

Generalizing about "Jews by choice" can be as dangerous as generalizing about Reform, Conservative, and Orthodox Judaism. There are "Jews by choice" who are rabbis, cantors, and educators; lecturers and authors. About the only thing that you might want to say is: People who study about Judaism know about Judaism; people who don't study about Judaism don't know about Judaism.

Why would anyone assume that "Jews by choice" knew less about Judaism than born Jews?

_____

_____

_____

_____

And now let's move on to Statement No. 3. Maybe it will give us a hint.

Statement No. 3: Unless you were born Jewish, you can never "really" be a Jew.
Answer: False.

Jewish tradition is quite clear in stating that one who converts to Judaism is to be considered a "Jewish newborn," entitled to an extra measure of love. Furthermore, we are told that we are not to remind those who choose Judaism that they were ever not Jewish. From the moment they convert to Judaism, they are Jewish!

What do we learn from this?

Fact No. 1: Many Jews do not know Jewish teachings regarding converts and should take time to acquaint themselves with these.

Fact No. 2: In Judaism, as in any other faith, there are those who genuinely feel that the only way to be a Jew is to be born a Jew—in spite of Jewish teachings.

Fact No. 3: There are many Jews who cannot understand why someone would choose to become a Jew. Therefore, they suspect or question those who do so.

Jews sometimes use two slang words to refer to non-Jews, usually in a derogatory way. The first word is "goy," literally meaning "nation" and originally a reference to the Israelites. The second word is "shiksa"—used to describe a non-Jewish woman—or "shaygetz"—used to describe a non-Jewish man. Most Jews do not know that these latter two words are derived from a Hebrew word meaning "abominable thing."

1. Now that you know the Jewish teaching regarding converts, do you feel it is important to end bias against those who have chosen Judaism?_____
   Why? _____

2. What can you do to end the use of words like "goy," "shiksa," and "shaygetz" by Jews you know?

   _____
   _____
   _____
   _____

 *Let's Review*

Thus far we have learned some interesting facts:

1. Judaism was once an active missionary faith. Only in relatively recent times have Jews discouraged missionary efforts and conversion.

2. It may indeed be that many of those who convert to Judaism know at least as much about Judaism as a result of their studies as do many born Jews.

3. Once an individual converts to Judaism, Jewish tradition considers that individual to be a Jew in every sense of the term.

4. The Union of American Hebrew Congregations has initiated an aggressive program of Outreach to new Jews, their families, and those who might ultimately wish to become Jews.

So far, so good. But now the going gets a little tougher!

Statement No. 4: Reform, Conservative, and Orthodox Jews basically agree on the requirements for conversion.
Answer: False.

Now we get to the most difficult issue of all. The whole issue of conversion involves far more than a debate over whether or not Jews should seek or welcome converts. It is not merely a matter of teaching Jewish sources or correcting faulty stereotypes. The issue of conversion involves a fundamental disagreement between Orthodoxy and Liberal Judaism.

What do we learn from this?

Fact No. 1: Orthodox Judaism recognizes only conversions performed before an Orthodox *bet din* (Jewish court comprising a panel of three Orthodox rabbis); requires *milah* (circumcision) for all male converts; requires ritual immersion in the *mikveh* (ritual bath) for men and women converting to Judaism; refuses to recognize as valid any conversion performed by a Reform or a Conservative rabbi, even if conducted before a *bet din* with *milah* for men and a visit to the *mikveh* for women and men.

Fact No. 2: Reform Judaism recognizes conversions performed by Orthodox, Conservative, and Reconstructionist, just as well as by Reform, rabbis; requires a period of intensive study as a precondition for conversion; views *mikveh* and *milah* as options but not as requirements for conversion.

> Why does Orthodox recognition of
> Reform conversions matter?

Orthodox recognition of a conversion is important only if the individual wishes to live in the State of Israel or must have an Orthodox rabbi officiate at the wedding. Because of the power of Orthodox political parties in Israel, the Orthodox rabbinate has thus far been able to define "acceptable" conversions in its own manner. This also has consequences on the lives of Jews living outside of Israel.

While an increase in the numbers of liberal Jews will ultimately neutralize Orthodoxy's influence, those now converting to Judaism who might want to make aliyah to Israel must know that their religious status will be questioned.

1. To help you understand the current power of Orthodoxy, consider the following. Let's say that you had been converted to Judaism by a Reform or Conservative rabbi. After six years you decide to move to Israel. You meet an Israeli, fall in love, and decide to marry. Since only Orthodox rabbis are legally allowed to officiate at weddings in Israel, you make an appointment for a premarital interview. During the course of your discussion, you mention your conversion. The rabbi immediately terminates the meeting, since you are not "Jewish" and he cannot officiate at intermarriages.

How do you react to this situation, which is fairly common in Israel today?

_____

_____

_____

What should the Reform and Conservative movements do to change the existing state of affairs?

_____

_____

_____

2. A Reform and an Orthodox rabbi recently proposed the formation of a joint *bet din* embracing all groups within the Jewish community. The idea was that such a group would standardize requirements for conversion to Judaism, including *milah* and *mikveh,* and thereby ensure universal acceptance of any individual's conversion. Do you feel that such a *bet din* is possible?_____ Why or why not? _____

_____

_____

Do you approve of the idea?_____ Why or why not? _____

_____

_____

Statement No. 5: Unless your mother was a Jew, you are not considered to be a born Jew.
Answer: True and false.

This last issue is a tough one and a little complicated. For at least the last 2,000 years or so, commonly accepted Jewish teaching has held that a child is automatically Jewish if his or her mother was Jewish. If your father was Jewish and your mother not, Jewish law held that you were not automatically a Jew.

In the eyes of Orthodoxy that definition still holds. If your mother is a Jew, you are a Jew. If not, you are not. So Statement No. 5 would be true if you were Orthodox.

In Reform Judaism, a child is Jewish if either parent is Jewish, provided the child is reared and educated as a Jew and becomes Bar/Bat Mitzvah or is confirmed. Reform views men and women as equal and the potential religious influence of either as sufficient.

How do you feel?

_____I agree with the CCAR position.

_____I disagree with the CCAR position.

Give the reasons for your choice.

_____

_____

_____

_____

ROUND SEVEN

About the Torah

Genesis 1:1–2:3 describes the different and separate stages of the creation of the world.

Review the order of creation as told in Genesis.

DAY

1. _____

2. _____

3. _____

4. _____

5. _____

6. _____

7. _____

How does this account of the creation of the world differ from the theories of creation that you studied in science? What do scientists think were the first steps in the creation process?

_____

_____

_____

_____

If you were asked to make a choice of which version of creation to believe in, which one would you choose? Be honest now. Don't choose one or the other because you think your teacher or rabbi expects a certain answer.

_____

_____

If you were an Orthodox Jew (or a fundamentalist Christian for that matter) chances are that you would choose the Bible version over the scientific approach. This would be in line with the Orthodox view that everything in the Bible is absolutely true and that God dictated the text of the entire Bible to Moses.

Some modern Orthodox Jews admit they have some difficulty believing the Genesis story. Here is what Rabbi J. David Bleich, a modern Orthodox scholar, wrote about these lines from Genesis:

> The biblical story of creation may be . . . difficult to understand. *Many Jews do not accept the theory of evolution.* (Emphasis ours). Those who do accept some aspects of evolution would speak, not of random occurrences or of the survival of the fittest, but of divine creation and a divinely guided evolutionary process. But even the most literalistic face the difficulty of explaining the phrase, "And it was evening and it was morning," which occurs in describing phases of creation which occurred prior to the creation of the sun and the moon. Remember that heavenly bodies were not created until the third day. But, then, to what does the word "day" refer when used in referring to the first days of creation? If there is no sun and no moon, what do the words "evening" and "morning" describe? Quite obviously, the reference is not to a day measured by sunset and sunrise. *The Torah is referring* to stages of creation. The use of the term "day," at least in this early period, is metaphorical. A metaphor is not a myth. It is not a "story" used to teach a moral, but a word

or phrase which has a meaning quite apart from its usual literal meaning. (From Borowitz, *Understanding Judaism,* UAHC.)

How do non-Orthodox Jews look upon the Bible if we do not believe it is the absolute truth—the literal word of God dictated to Moses? For us, the Torah and the rest of the Bible are a record of the searching of people to find God. Since the Bible, in the opinion of liberal Judaism, was written over many generations, it contains many different ideas. Some of them reflect the beliefs of the people among whom Jews lived. Others are a record of various attempts to understand the world.

The Jews were not the only ones who tried to understand how the world came to be. Here is another ancient creation story from an Akkadian epic dating about 2000 B.C.E.

> Then the lord (Marduk) paused to view her (Tiamat's)
>   dead body,
> That he might divide the monster and do artful works.
> He split her like a shellfish into two parts:
> Half of her he set up and ceiled it as a sky,
> Pulled down the bar and posted guards.
> He bade them to allow not her waters to escape,
> He crossed the heavens and surveyed its regions. . . .
> He constructed nations for the great gods,
> Fixing their astral likenesses as constellations. . . .
> In her (Tiamat's) belly he established the zenith.
> The moon he caused to shine, the night to him
>   enthrusting.
> (Marduk reveals his plan to create man)
> Blood I will mass and cause bones to be.
> I will establish a savage, "man" shall be his name.
> Verily, savage man I will create.
> He shall be charged with the service of the gods that
>   they might be at ease! (From "Enuma Elish,"
>   *Ancient Near Eastern Texts,* ed. James B. Pritchard.)

Can you accept Rabbi Bleich's interpretation? What are the basic differences between the biblical version of creation and the Akkadian version?

_____

_____

_____

_____

You might say that the biblical version is more familiar; you might say that it is a bit less gory. From a scientific viewpoint, neither story can be described as terribly accurate.

Now, go back and reread Genesis 1:1–2:3.

Clearly a very important difference is a moral, ethical dimension central to the biblical version, contrasting with the many other early attempts to figure out how the universe came to be.

Another major difference is the idea of rest—God rested after laboring for six days.

Is the importance of the Torah lessened because every word is not absolutely true?

Liberal Jews believe not. In fact, the acceptance of the Bible as a history of the Jews striving to find God sets the Bible on a higher level. We see the high minded and noble reaching for something beyond themselves.

ROUND EIGHT

On Living an Ethical Life

It's interesting how we Jews become upset when we read newspaper accounts of other Jews who have been accused or convicted of crimes.

This story from the *Jerusalem Post* (as told by an Orthodox rabbi, L. I. Rabinowitz) is an example.

> In July, 1979, a sensational case of gold smuggling into Israel was exposed by the police. The arch-smuggler was a veteran pilot of El Al with a distinguished flying record to his credit. It was he who brought the last consignment of gold bricks, in the possession of which he was apprehended, to the apartment . . . where the police lay in ambush, waiting for other participants in the alleged crime to assemble. They swooped down on the apartment, and among those who were caught in the net were two young men, members of the fanatically Orthodox Jewish sect which inhabits the Meah Shearim Quarter of Jerusalem. When surprised, the men attempted to make their escape by fleeing in a car but were hotly pursued by the police, who had to fire at the tires in order to bring the car to a halt and to arrest them. This bizarre detail of what has been a massive, well-organized criminal activity which has been going on for years, and whose ramifications have not yet been fully revealed, was, of course, prominently featured in the local press and resulted in the following letter which appeared in the English language *Jerusalem Post* of July 25:

> Sir, when you reported on the diamond (sic) smuggling incident (July 17), it was wrong of you to single out two of the suspects by describing them as "men from Jerusalem's ultra-Orthodox Meah Shearim." You did not de-

scribe the other suspects as being nonreligious and, from nonreligious neighborhoods, if this is so. If these two Meah Shearim people are guilty, their guilt has nothing to do with their supposed piety.

Do you agree with the writer of the letter that the Orthodoxy of the young men had nothing to do with their being accused of smuggling?_____
Explain your answer.

_____

_____

What does being religious really mean?

With your classmates, rate the following items on a scale of 1 to 10, with 10 being the "most religious" activity and 1 being the "least religious."

_____ Keeping kosher.

_____ Attending Sabbath services on a regular basis.

_____ Not stealing.

_____ Not lying.

_____ Honoring your father and mother.

_____ Wearing a *kipah* all the time.

_____ Not working on Saturday.

_____ Lighting Shabbat candles every Friday evening.

_____ Not cheating.

_____ Fasting on Yom Kippur.

The prophet Isaiah had a few things to say about being religious:

They ask of Me the right way, as though eager for the nearness of God. "When we fast," you say, "why do You pay no heed? Why, when we afflict ourselves, do You take no notice?"

Because on your fast day you think only of your business, and oppress all your workers! Because your fasting leads only to strife and discord, and hitting out with a cruel fist! Such a way of fasting on this day will not help you to be heard on high.

Is this the fast I look for? A day of self-affliction? Bowing your head like a reed, and covering yourself with sackcloth and ashes? Is not this the fast I look for: to unlock the shackles of injustice, to undo the fetters of bondage, to let the oppressed go free, and to break every cruel chain? Is it not to share your bread with the hungry, and to bring the homeless poor into your house? When you see the naked, to clothe them, and never to hide yourself from your own kin?

Then shall your light blaze forth like the dawn and your wounds shall quickly heal; your Righteous One will walk before you, and the Presence of the Lord will be your rear guard. Then, when you call, the Lord will answer; when you cry, God will say: "Here I am . . . ." (Isaiah 58:2–9)

After having read what the prophet Isaiah wrote, go back and consider again the order of items "most religious" and "least religious." Would you change the order now?

The report of the smuggling incident in Israel and the challenge of the prophet Isaiah are examples of two extremes in the Jewish world today. There are, indeed, a few Jews, as the newspaper article illustrates, who pay attention exclusively to the details of ritual law as laid out in the *Shulchan Aruch,* a code of observances assembled by Joseph Karo in the sixteenth century, and ignore the ethical precepts of the prophets. There are other Jews who pay absolutely no attention to ritual and observe only the ethical principles.

Most Jews are not at one end of this scale or the other, but some place in between. We choose those rituals which have meaning for us today, ignoring others. But the ethical principles of Judaism are always meaningful.

 We all need reminders to help us keep the ethical basis of Judaism clearly in mind. In a sense, the rituals are signposts along the road to an ethical life. Even if a highway is very familiar, without a road sign we may wonder if we've passed an exit or absent-mindedly made a wrong turn.

Jews at the end of the scale have lost the meaning of Judaism as an ethical way of life, despite their zeal to observe every detail of the rules and regulations laid out in *halachah* (Jewish law). For them, the signs became more important than the road.

Early Reform Jews, in rebelling against such an emphasis in Judaism, paid no attention to ritual. In their way, they went to extremes too, ignoring the signs.

Reform Jews today are trying to strike a balance between the two extremes. They choose rituals which:
  · help to remind them that they are Jews;
  · help them to identify with other Jews and feel part of the Jewish community;
  · help them to learn anew and to remember the ethical ideas that Judaism teaches.

Think of the Reform, Conservative, and Orthodox Jews you know and list (on the following chart) the differences that you see in their ritual observances.

Reform Jews	Conservative Jews	Orthodox Jews

Orthodox Jews regard every letter, word, sentence, and paragraph of the Bible as absolute truth, the unalterable word of God. Equal in ritualistic importance to Orthodox Jews are the Mishnah and the Gemarah of the Talmud, known as the Oral Law. Although written over many centuries in different countries, each rule is as important as every other.

For the rest of us, the difference is not in our understanding the ethical ideas of Judaism and the importance of living by them but rather in the emphasis we place on the observance of rituals which help us remember to put ethical ideas into practice.

What are the real differences?

In the preceding pages, we've described a number of

issues which conceivably could divide Reform, Conservative, and Orthodox Jews.

For each of the issues listed below, decide for yourself (or in small groups) whether these issues are extremely divisive; fairly divisive; not too divisive; not at all divisive.

	Extremely divisive	Fairly divisive	Not too divisive	Not at all divisive
Yarmulkes				
Beards				
Talit and tefilin				
"G-d"				
Women				
Bat Mitzvah				
"Jews by choice"				
The Torah				
Ethics				

Now discuss your individual and group answers as a class.

Well, what did you find? Are there any issues that are irresolvable? If not, how might one or all of the groups modify their position—without sacrificing their integrity—to attain Jewish unity? Are there many issues that separate us as Jews? Or are the similarities greater than the differences? Will the conflicts prevent us from agreeing on everything? Is such agreement necessary? Desirable?

Tough questions! But don't give up. More help is on the way!

UNIT III

Getting Closer Together

ROUND ONE

> Are Reform, Conservative, and Orthodox Judaism becoming more "alike" and, if so, which is becoming more like which?

Interview a Reform, a Conservative, and an Orthodox rabbi and ask them the following two questions:
1. Are the other two branches of Judaism becoming more like your own, or is yours becoming more like one or both of the others?
2. Whichever it is, in what areas?
   Record the interviews or make notes of the answers.
   On the following checklist, put a check mark (√) in each column for the topics the rabbis came up with and an asterisk (*) for the topics you bring up. You may add to the checklist any other topics you, your group, or your teacher would suggest.

	Reform	Conservative	Orthodox
Israel			
Aliyah			
Organizations national			
regional			
local			
men's			
women's			
youth's			
Worship services			
Sermon			
Prayer book			
English in prayer			
Bar Mitzvah			
Bat Mitzvah			
Confirmation			
Wedding			
Jewish education			
Mixed seating			
Mixed choir			
Kashrut			
Shabbat observance			
Holiday observance			
Ideas about God			
Jewish people			
Judaism			

Now prepare a report covering the three interviews.
    Other activities would be:
1. Play back the taped interviews to the class and discuss your checklist.
2. Design a large poster similar to the suggested checklist, listing the answers you got, with arrows pointing from one column to another, to show who is imitating whom according to each rabbi.
3. Act out a discussion among the three rabbis. The actors shouldn't simply repeat the statements of the rabbis interviewed, but they should play their roles realistically and engage in a vigorous, give-and-take discussion.

A leading American rabbi and Jewish scholar says the various branches of Judaism are growing more and more alike all the time. Assuming that is true, and that you agree with the statement, consider the following three possible causes that may bring about such a trend.
    · General American influences and attitudes.
    · Zionism and the State of Israel.
    · The Nazi holocaust.
Can you explain how each of these factors tends to make the different branches of Judaism more and more alike?

_____

_____

_____

_____

_____

Can you think of other causes, factors, reasons behind such a trend?

_____

_____

_____

_____

Against such a trend?

_____

_____

_____

_____

Do you agree or disagree with the rabbi?

_____

_____

ROUND TWO

What do we mean by "alike"? Does it mean "the same" or "identical"?

"Alike" means that:
- · things are similar in many ways but not necessarily in *all* ways.
- · the similarities are so great and so important that they could outweigh the differences.

> Are the similarities between Reform, Conservative, and Orthodox Judaism so great and so important that they outweigh the differences?

In your opinion, would a merger of Reform, Conservative, and Orthodox be:

_____ impossible;

_____ very hard;

_____ not too difficult;

_____ pretty easy;

_____ very easy.

Many years ago, the Jewish Theological Seminary, which trains Conservative rabbis, awarded an honorary doctor of philosophy degree to an outstanding Jewish scholar for his exceptional learning and genius. Was this scholar Reform, Conservative, or Orthodox?_____

And now here's the answer: The scholar was Kaufmann Kohler, president of the Hebrew Union College—the Reform rabbinical seminary!

What's in a Name?

A few years ago, the president of a Reform temple urged publicly that the name "Reform Judaism" should be changed because it didn't relate to the dictionary definition of "reform." A Jewish newspaper editor who was not Reform made this angry reply:

> Reform Judaism, just like Conservatism and Orthodoxy, is faced with a life and death struggle. The issues are numerous and profound, and the needs great. But none has the faintest connection with nomenclature (names).

When there's so much else to be done, the editor added, why make "a federal case" out of "such a picayune point"? In other words, as Shakespeare put it, "What's in a name?" Look up "reform" in your own dictionary and then take a stand.

The name of a religious movement, like Reform, Conservative, or Orthodox:

_____is unimportant and makes no difference in understanding what the movement is all about;

_____is somewhat important and makes some difference;

_____is very important and makes a big difference.

Now let's look into this matter of names a bit more carefully and see whether you would want to change your answers.

Facts You Should Know about "Reform":
Not all Reform groups use the name "reform." Great Britain, for example, has a "Union of Liberal and Progressive Synagogues," not "Reform." Look up "progressive" and "liberal" in your dictionary. Are they really different from "reform"? Which do you prefer?

The international organization of Reform synagogues calls itself the "World Union for Progressive Judaism." The national organization of Reform temples in the United States and Canada doesn't even use the word "reform": it's called "Union of American Hebrew Congregations." The Hebrew Union College-Jewish Institute of Religion (the seminary that trains Reform rabbis, cantors, and educators), the Central Conference of American Rabbis (national organization of Reform rabbis), the National Association of Temple Educators (organization of Reform educators), and the American Conference of Cantors (organization of Reform cantors) have no "Reform" in their names.

Many Reform Jews don't like the term "reform" and what it implies. It was all right, they say, when the Reform movement began. The early "reformers" wanted to modernize Judaism, drop or change certain "out-of-date" practices and beliefs, add new ones, make certain adjustments and "improvements." But, by now, all the "reform" has taken place. The only thing the Reform movement seems to be "reforming" today is itself. What makes Reform Judaism different is that it is more liberal (more willing to make changes, to allow more diversity) and more progressive (constantly changing and improving itself). Some Reform Jews today have reintroduced a number of traditional practices. So, these Reform Jews argue, let's call our movement Liberal Judaism or Progressive Judaism and forget about "Reform."

Facts You Should Know about "Conservative":
Not all Conservative Jews like their name either. Their national organization (United Synagogue of America), their national rabbinical body (Rabbinical Assembly of America), and their seminary for training rabbis (Jewish Theological Seminary) also avoid the term "conservative." (An interesting sidelight: the Seminary originally planned to have "Orthodox" in its name but changed it to "Jewish.")

Facts You Should Know about "Orthodox":
Many Orthodox Jews, too, object to their name. The term "orthodox" was first applied by the French Sanhedrin (an assembly of Jewish leaders convened by Napoleon). It was later used by Samson Raphael Hirsch to differentiate between traditionalist and Reform Jews. Many Orthodox Jews prefer the term "Torah-true Jews." The foremost Orthodox rabbinical seminary (Isaac Elchanan Theological Seminary) and rabbinical body (Rabbinical Council of America) similarly avoid the term "orthodox."

Let's return to the dictionary definition.
Here's an example from a college dictionary. Compare it with your own dictionary.

Reform: change for the better, improvement, correcting faults.

That fits what early reformers were trying to do—and what Reform Jews are trying to do today.

Conservative: gradual change and reform based on historical development consistent with the basic principles of Jewish law.

Orthodox: acceptance of ideas and practices as set forth in *halachah* (law).

Think of a better name for:
- · Reform Judaism_____
- · Conservative Judaism_____
- · Orthodox Judaism_____

Tally everyone's answers in a class opinion poll and send them to the school paper, to a national leader, or to a national organization.

Does arriving at a definition resolve the difficulty?____

Now that you have examined the problem, do you still feel the same way about the importance or non-importance of a religious movement's name? If important—why? If not important—why not?

_____
_____
_____
_____

ROUND THREE

A Matter of Time

You are taken blindfolded to a synagogue on Friday night or Shabbat morning for exactly five minutes. Could you tell, before your five minutes are up, whether you are in a Reform, Conservative, or Orthodox synagogue?_____
Why or why not?

_____

_____

When you've worked this out, one way or the other, try the same problem for a religious school classroom.

Could you tell which kind of religious school it is?____
Why or why not?

_____

_____

If you decided you could not do either of these things in five minutes, ask yourself how long it would take you—and why!

_____

_____

Is there actually a "yes" or "no" answer to these questions? Did you write "maybe" or "don't know"? Did you change your answers when you gave yourself more than five minutes? Did you mention some specific part of the service or the lesson that could identify the situation for you?

If you did any of these things, you're catching on—as actually the whole situation was a set up for some new traps.

One trap is in the "five minutes." If you say that's enough time, you're really saying that Reform, Conservative, and Orthodox are so utterly different in synagogue and classroom that it wouldn't matter when you arrived or how long you stayed or when you left. You're saying that any five minutes would do because the difference would be obvious right away.

But it just isn't so. A congregation might be singing the hymn, *Yigdal,* in Hebrew in the traditional melody, or the *Shema* in Hebrew, or the *Kiddush.* Then you couldn't tell if you were in a Reform, Conservative, or Orthodox synagogue. The class might be drilling some point in Hebrew grammar or learning an Israeli song. Again you couldn't tell. The Torah reading might give it away, or the sermon, or in the classroom a discussion about a holiday or kosher food. Your five minutes might tell you it was not an Orthodox synagogue or classroom, but not whether it was Reform or Conservative; or that it was not Reform, but not whether it was Conservative or Orthodox.

So, you see, it would matter a great deal which five minutes you observed. Similarity and difference, here, could be a matter of time.

The second trap involves the words "alike" and "different" which were not used in the situation but which were an important part of it just the same. If two congregations both chant a certain prayer in Hebrew, while standing, but to different melodies; or if one chants it and the other merely reads it; or if one recites it in Hebrew, another in English, and still another in both languages—are these congregations "alike" in their worship or "different"?

In your five minutes, you might hear something you consider "different" from your own synagogue and decide that this synagogue belongs to a different branch of Judaism.

Other people might decide the synagogue belongs to the same branch, with just a few small differences of its own.

You might hear something in the classroom that would probably never come up in your own religious school—is it the same type of school as yours, with a few "small differences of its own," or a different type of school altogether?

How "alike" do things have to be to be the same? How "different" do they have to be to be different?

How long do you think it would take you, blindfolded, to tell whether you are in a synagogue or a church? In a Jewish or Christian religious school?

1. One way to check out your ideas about all this is for you or a group to attend a service in your own synagogue and in two other synagogues of the two other branches. Watch especially for times in the service when:
    · all three are enough "alike" so you couldn't pass the blindfold test in those few minutes;
    · things are so "different" you could pass the blindfold test in five minutes;
    · two are enough "alike" but the third is very "different."

    One or two examples of each will be enough. You're not trying to actually pass a blindfold test—only to become more alert to "alike" and "different."

2. Another way to check out your ideas is for you or a group to find out how "alike" or "different" the official Reform, Conservative, and Orthodox prayer books are. Consult the following:

- *Gates of Prayer,* Central Conference of American Rabbis, 1975 (Reform).
- *Union Prayer Book,* Central Conference of American Rabbis, 1940 (Reform).
- *Sabbath and Festival Prayer Book,* Rabbinical Assembly of America and United Synagogue of America, 1946 (Conservative).
- *The Siddur,* Rabbinical Council of America, 1960 (Orthodox).

Look for one or two examples, each, of:

- prayers or services that are "alike";
- prayers or services that are pretty much alike, with only slight differences;
- prayers or services that are definitely "different." (For example, a prayer or service in one book but not in the other is a definite difference; so is a prayer given in full in one book but very much shortened in another; and how about a prayer that's in Hebrew in one book, in English in another, in both languages in the third!)

Either of these projects—and certainly both of them—will take you a little time. Plan to report on them to the class. By that time, you'll be a lot surer of yourself and the class discussion and questions should be rather interesting.

ROUND FOUR

A Grammar Lesson

Definition No. 1: Judaism—noun naming a belief or faith or way of life.
Definition No. 2: Reform, Conservative, Orthodox—adjectives modifying or limiting or describing the noun Judaism.

> Which is more important—the adjective or the noun? The "Reform," "Conservative," or "Orthodox" or the "Judaism"?

Before you make up your mind on this, let's try a few other "arrangements":

1. How about dropping the noun and using the adjective all by itself?
    · Reform believes that. . . .
    · Conservative stands for. . . .
    · Orthodox opposes. . . .
    (Right now, it doesn't matter how the sentence ends.)
    How is this way of talking?
    ＿＿＿＿better;
    ＿＿＿＿worse;
    ＿＿＿＿not different.
    Why? ＿＿＿＿＿＿＿＿＿＿＿＿＿＿＿＿＿＿＿＿
    ＿＿＿＿＿＿＿＿＿＿＿＿＿＿＿＿＿＿＿＿＿＿＿＿
    ＿＿＿＿＿＿＿＿＿＿＿＿＿＿＿＿＿＿＿＿＿＿＿＿

2. How about dropping the adjective and adding a qualifying phrase to the noun?
   · Judaism, according to the Reform view, believes. . . .
   · Judaism, according to the Conservative view, stands for. . . .
   · Judaism, according to the Orthodox view, opposes. . . .
   (Here again, the ending doesn't matter.)
   How is this way of talking?
   _____better;
   _____worse;
   _____not different.
3. How about inserting another noun plus a preposition?
   · The Reform movement in Judaism believes. . . .
   · The Conservative movement in Judaism stands for. . . .
   · The Orthodox movement in Judaism opposes. . . .
   How is this way of talking?
   _____better;
   _____worse;
   _____not different.

> Reform and Conservative Jews often add the word "movement"; Orthodox Jews never do—they say "Orthodoxy" or "Orthodox Judaism." Why?

4. How about playing around with capital letters? For instance:
   · Reform JUDAISM vs. REFORM Judaism.
   · Conservative JUDAISM vs. CONSERVATIVE Judaism

· Orthodox JUDAISM vs. ORTHODOX Judaism.
Or: Changing capitals to small letters.
· reform Judaism vs. Reform judaism.
· conservative Judaism vs. Conservative judaism.
· orthodox Judaism vs. Orthodox Judaism.
Never mind the rules of capitalization; just try saying all these terms out loud, emphasizing the words with capitals, underemphasizing the words with small letters.

Considering both the way the words look to your eyes and the way they sound, would it be a good idea to change our way of writing and printing them?_____
Why? _____

_____

5. How about our way of thinking about them? Shall we change that?_____
Why? _____

_____

Now, check (✓) the statement with which you agree:
_____The adjective (Reform, Conservative, Orthodox) is more important than the noun (Judaism).
_____The noun (Judaism) is more important than the adjective (Reform, Conservative, Orthodox).
Take a poll of your classmates to determine the majority opinion.
If your personal answer was different from the majority answer, do you want to go back and change your personal answer?
_____Yes, because _____

_____

_____No, because _____

_____Not sure, because _____

Was there a trap here?_____
Why? _____
_____

You had a choice between two answers—but isn't there a third?
Try it again, now, with the third possibility.
_____The adjective (Reform, Conservative, Orthodox) is more important than the noun (Judaism).
_____The noun (Judaism) is more important than the adjective (Reform, Conservative, Orthodox).
_____The noun (Judaism) is just as important as the adjective (Reform, Conservative, Orthodox).
Again, what is the class majority opinion? Write it here:
_____
_____

And, again, do you want to change your own answer?
_____Yes, because _____

_____No, because _____

_____Not sure, because _____

Did you notice this trap before I mentioned it? If you did, congratulations!

If you didn't, be more careful next time.

Consider the question first, before you try to answer it. Remind yourself about guessing and "don't know" and "not sure" and about stereotypes and faulty generalizations and hidden assumptions. And, above all, look for traps!

What difference does all this grammar-and-capitalization make?

What we're really talking about, here, of course, isn't grammar or capitalization at all—but about whether Reform, Conservative, and Orthodox:

_____a. are more alike than they are different;

_____b. are more different than they are alike;

_____c. have similarities that are more important than the differences;

_____d. have differences that are more important than the similarities.

What do you think? Check your opinion. You're allowed only two checks—a or b; c or d. Make a double check if the class majority agrees with you.

Finally: If you checked a or c, put down here two or three main similarities that you see among Reform, Conservative, and Orthodox:

1. _____
2. _____
3. _____

But now if you checked b or d, look back at the very first start where you had listed the main differences among Reform, Conservative, and Orthodox. How do you feel about the answers you gave then? Do you want to change what you wrote there?

Fill in accordingly:

_____I would still write the same differences as at the start.

_____I would change these differences now, as follows:

1. _____
2. _____
3. _____

ROUND FIVE
Plus and Minus

Don't get the idea that all Reform, Conservative, and Orthodox Jews are friendly, tolerant, and understanding of one another. There's also plenty of bad feeling, scorn, mockery, and unfair criticism. It is important to recognize the difference between a plus and a minus.

Differences You Should Learn:

Plus	Minus
Honest disagreement.	Prejudice.
Constructive criticism with appreciation of the best in someone you oppose.	Unfair attack, picking on the worst in someone you oppose.
Opinion based on knowledge and understanding.	Opinion based on ignorance and misunderstanding.
Willingness to work with others, stressing similarities without ignoring differences.	Refusing to work with others, stressing differences and ignoring similarities.

R Be able to help others understand Judaism—your branch and others—when it is misunderstood or attacked out of prejudice, unfairness, or ignorance. Learn to correct your own wrong ideas and unfair statements.

Let's get some practice making distinctions.

Some of the following authentic statements are honest, constructive, understanding, and cooperative. Others are prejudiced, unfair, destructive, and divisive.

Put a plus sign (+) beside the constructive and a minus sign (−) beside the destructive statements.

_____ 1. A leading Orthodox scholar was asked by Orthodox rabbis if, according to traditional Jewish law, they could accept membership on a rabbinic committee that also has Reform or Conservative rabbis on it. After long and careful study, the reply was "yes."

_____ 2. When this Orthodox scholar gave his answer, the heads of eleven Orthodox yeshivot (talmudic academies) still said no.

_____ 3. An Orthodox Yiddish novelist, after visiting the Hebrew Union College-Jewish Institute of Religion (Reform) which trains Reform rabbis, praised its Jewishness, talmudic studies, learning, and devotion to Judaism.

_____ 4. A Yiddish writer said, "An atheist rabbi is hardly an exception in Reform Judaism."

_____ 5. An outstanding Orthodox rabbi declared, "We cannot withdraw ourselves from the Jewish community. Orthodoxy is not only for the Orthodox."

_____ 6. A Reform rabbi, in a widely quoted sermon, described Orthodoxy as the "medieval vestige [remainder] of ghettoized life."

_____7. A Reform rabbi delivered a Rosh Hashanah sermon called, "Are Traditional Jewish Ideas Dead?" in which he explained and endorsed four basic Orthodox religious ideas.

_____8. An Orthodox rabbi said that, wherever the Reform movement grows, intermarriage also increases.

_____9. A prominent Conservative rabbi pointed out that the Conservative movement has to move decisively in shaping a Conservative *halachah:* "One that each rabbi, synagogue, and layman would adhere to or else they would be expected to leave the movement."

_____10. Some Orthodox rabbis refuse money for their institutions from local federations of Jewish philanthropies saying, "Reform and Conservative rabbis have too much influence on your board of directors."

_____11. The Union of Orthodox Rabbis of the United States and Canada notified kosher butchers and caterers that "individuals and organizations adhering to the Conservative and Reform movements are not competent to practice the rabbinate in any function whatever."

Here are some facts about the three branches of Judaism:

Orthodox Jews look upon their faith as the mainstream of a tradition that has been steadfast and unaltered for the past three thousand years. They accept biblical law as the revealed will of God and believe with equal fervor in what they call the Oral Law—the traditional interpretation of the Mosaic Law as embodied in the Talmud and other legal codes.

Reform or Liberal Jews accept as binding only moral laws of the Bible and those ceremonies that "elevate and sanctify our lives." They do not abide by those customs that "are not adapted to the views and habits of modern civilization."

Conservative Jews follow the pattern of traditional Judaism, by and large, but believe that "Jewish law, like every other living manifestation, must necessarily grow if it is to remain alive. They feel that change should be the result of natural growth and in consonance with the spirit of Jewish law."

Do you consider the above facts honest, fair, constructive, and understanding? Give your reasons.

_____

_____

_____

_____

Now back to the eleven statements. Here's how I rate them:
Plus: 1, 3, 5, 7, 9.
Minus: 2, 4, 6, 8, 10, 11.

If you, your classmates, or your teacher don't agree with my answers, talk over those statements and decide whether you still believe your answers were right or you want to change them.

Let's study a little deeper some of these statements to see what we can learn.

Statement No. 1: What kind of institution needs a "mixed" rabbinic committee? In such an institution, who suffers when one group of rabbis refuses to participate? The participants? The non-participants? All of them?

Statement No. 2: If your community has a board of rabbis representing Reform, Conservative, Orthodox, and perhaps even Reconstructionist branches, find out how long it has been in existence, how it operates, examples of its success and failure, your own rabbi's opinion of its value, other questions of your own.

Statement No. 10: Who is hurt most by this attitude? If your community has a Jewish welfare federation, find out its exact name, whether all kinds of Jews are on its board (Reform, Conservative, Orthodox, and Reconstructionist), whether it gives funds to all kinds of institutions, whether all branches are represented and get the same treatment (if not, find out why and what could be done about it).

Statement No. 7: The four basic Orthodox religious ideas that the Reform rabbi endorsed are (a) their objection to abortion, with limited exceptions, based on what the Orthodox understand as a religious command in Genesis 1:28 (look it up!); (b) their support of US government aid to Jewish day schools (many are almost bankrupt and will close without such aid; however, most Reform rabbis want complete separation of church and state, which for them means no government aid to religious schools); (c) their belief in life after death for our souls and the resurrection of our bodies at the coming of the Messiah (as this belief has a strong and comforting emotional appeal, giving life meaning and purpose); (d) their belief in a personal, human Messiah or deliverer (this belief implies that people don't act alone, but God can and must act, too, in contrast to the Reform idea that we are co-partners with God in bringing about the messianic age).

1. Interview your teacher, parents, principal, school board chairperson, rabbi and find out their reactions toward the four ideas discussed above. Now, interview principals, chairpersons, rabbis of a different branch of Judaism. Then, report to the class your findings pointing out where most agreed with you.

2. What do you—or your parents—usually mean by the term "religious"? Check one:

    _____Outward actions such as rituals, political positions, dress, food, and language?

    _____Inner faith and values such as love for Jewish tradition, commitment, covenant, belief that life has meaning, sincere feelings about God?

And now let's analyze your answers.

Those who check "Outward" generally end up describing an Orthodox Jew rather than a Reform or Conservative

Jew: "I'm not religious," they say. "I don't put on *tefilin* or pray three times a day or eat kosher. . . ." They are defining religion almost entirely as practices, customs, rituals. If you observe certain customs, you are "religious." If you don't keep these customs, you are "not religious."

Those who check "Inner" generally end up describing a religious Jew—who may be Reform, Conservative, or Orthodox. "I'm religious," they say. "I care about my ancestors and identify with their beliefs. I think there's a meaning and purpose to life and Judaism helps me figure out what it is and how to work for it. I believe in God and that God helps us." They are defining "religious" almost entirely as ideas, values, concepts. If you accept these ideas and try to live by them, you are "religious." If you don't accept them you are "not religious."

Both are important, of course—customs and ideas. In fact, one without the other doesn't make much sense. But the point I'm really making here is that a ritual definition of religion leads you to talk about things peculiar to Orthodox Jews, whereas a spiritual definition of religion leads you to talk about things common to Reform, Conservative, and Orthodox Jews—all "religious" Jews.

Conclusion: What distinguishes Reform, Conservative, and Orthodox Judaism from one another today is mainly practice, custom, and ritual. What unites Reform, Conservative, and Orthodox Jews are ideas, values, and concepts. What do you think of my conclusion? Check one and give your reasons:

_____I agree because _____

_____

_____I disagree because _____

_____

_____I'm not sure because _____

_____

℞ Though the solution is difficult, we should not shirk the responsibility of trying to find one. In religious school, at home, in public school, in synagogue, try to go beyond what people say, try to understand what kind of people they are, what they do or seem to think and figure out their "Inner" ideas, values, and concepts. Weigh them, accept or reject them—instead of the "Outward" things. Now try to understand yourself and your "Inner" ideas and weigh them.

1. Does the Conservative rabbi in Statement No. 9 oppose the two "extremes" of Reform and Orthodoxy? Does he want to abolish them? Does he want to change them? (Hint: If he did, what would happen to the "middle link"?)

2. Do you think Reform and Orthodoxy are very far apart? What are some beliefs, ideas, or actions about which Reform and Orthodoxy might agree?

   _____

   _____

   _____

3. Does this Conservative rabbi see Judaism as three separate boxes where you must get into one or the other or as a three-car train with doors connecting the cars so that you can move around from car to car?
   Which is your picture of Judaism? Check one:
   _____boxes;
   _____a train of cars.

The next is a tricky question—watch out!
How do Reform Jews picture Judaism?
_____boxes;
_____a train of cars.
How do Conservative?
_____boxes;
_____a train of cars.
How do Orthodox?
_____boxes;
_____a train of cars.
Did you answer? You shouldn't have! There are some Reform, Conservative, and Orthodox Jews who think of Judaism as three separate boxes. And there are other Reform, Conservative, and Orthodox Jews who think of Judaism as three (or more) cars of a train.

If you picture Judaism as a train of cars, what is the engine? Would Conservative Judaism apparently represent the middle car? Which would be the first car, Reform or Orthodoxy? How would Reform, Conservative, and Orthodox Jews answer these questions?

While others disagree, some Orthodox rabbis in the Rabbinical Council of America want the organization officially to refuse to recognize marriages or conversions performed by Reform or Conservative rabbis, even if the ceremony strictly follows all Orthodox rules and requirements. These Orthodox rabbis consider a religious ceremony valid only if performed by an Orthodox rabbi and under Orthodox control.

1. Interview an Orthodox rabbi who holds the policy stated above and ask him to defend his point of view.
2. Interview an Orthodox rabbi who disagrees with such a policy and ask him to explain why.
3. In your opinion, do Reform, Conservative, and Orthodox Judaism represent different religions, different kinds of Judaism, or just different organizations representing pretty much the same kind of Judaism? Is one of them "true Judaism" and are the others "dissenters"? Explain your point of view.

_____

_____

_____

_____

4. Write to the Rabbinical Council of America asking what their official stand is on marriage, conversion, and divorce performed by a Reform or a Conservative rabbi.
5. Consider the following statements and decide whether they are a plus or a minus. How do you as a Reform or Conservative Jew feel about them? Indicate your an-

swers using the following code: (a) angry; (b) puzzled; (c) sympathetic; or (d) understanding.

_____Some Orthodox rabbis refuse to call their Reform and Conservative colleagues "rabbi."

_____Some Orthodox rabbis will not allow Reform or Conservative rabbis to participate in wedding ceremonies or sign the *ketubah* (marriage document).

_____There are two Jewish-sponsored universities in the United States. One of them, an Orthodox institution, prefers to honor Christians or non-religious Jews rather than Reform or Conservative Jews.

_____At nearly every convention of the Rabbinical Council of America (Orthodox), a resolution is presented to withdraw from the Synagogue Council of America (Reform, Conservative, Orthodox): it is always overwhelmingly defeated.

_____The Rabbinical Council of America had a sharp internal quarrel when its convention committee invited a Conservative and a Reform rabbi to speak on the program. Some members said, "Non-Orthodox rabbis have no place lecturing Orthodox rabbis at a rabbinical council meeting."

_____An Orthodox alumnus sharply criticized the Yeshiva University (Orthodox) for awarding an honorary degree to another Orthodox alumnus who is the rabbi of a Conservative synagogue.

ROUND SIX

Statistics

In a large city, Jews of different branches were polled on the following two questions:

· Do you consider yourself Reform, Conservative, or Orthodox?

· Do you belong to a synagogue, and, if so, what kind?

One out of ten who were members of Reform congregations said: "I am not Reform."

One out of ten who were members of Conservative congregations said: "I am not Conservative."

One out of three who were members of Orthodox congregations said: "I am not Orthodox."

Nine out of ten who were not members of any synagogue said they were Reform, Conservative, or Orthodox.

Why do people join a synagogue when they do not consider themselves belonging to the branch of Judaism it stands for?

_____

_____

_____

Why do so many people who do not join any kind of congregation call themselves Reform, Conservative, or Orthodox?

_____

_____

_____

Why only one-tenth of Reform and Conservative synagogue members do not consider themselves Reform or Conservative, whereas one-third of Orthodox synagogue members do not consider themselves Orthodox?

_____

_____

_____

_____

Make a Guess

Which religious school—Reform, Conservative, or Orthodox—includes in its curriculum more courses about the other two branches? Write MANY, SOME, or NONE in each blank below:

_____ Reform religious schools have courses on Conservative and Orthodox Judaism.

_____ Conservative schools have courses on Reform and Orthodoxy.

_____ Orthodox schools have courses on Reform and Conservative Judaism.

Assuming you are right, and the three groups differ as you have indicated, how would you explain why one group has many such courses, another some, or none?

_____

_____

_____

_____

Facts You Should Know:

· Many Reform religious schools have regular courses in comparative Judaism where students learn about the Conservative and the Orthodox branches. The

Union of American Hebrew Congregations has, in fact, published this volume on comparative Judaism to help in such courses.

· A few Conservative schools have such courses as well.

· No Orthodox schools I know of have such courses, however.

1. Why do you think Reform religious schools are generally more eager to teach about Conservative and Orthodox Judaism than the other way around? Why do you think some Reform religious schools engage teachers who are Conservative or Orthodox, but Conservative and Orthodox religious schools do not hire teachers who are Reform? Is all this a sign of strength or weakness in Reform Judaism?

_____

_____

_____

_____

2. Write or phone to find out about such courses in other religious schools of your community. Report your findings to the class. Does your community have courses for adults and/or teachers on all three branches of Judaism?

_____

_____

_____

_____

3. Answer the following questions by checking each YES or NO.

_____Has your class—or any class in your religious school—ever visited a synagogue or a religious school of another branch of Judaism?

_____Has your class or any other class ever had visitors from a different branch of Judaism?

_____students;

_____adults.

_____Has your class ever had a joint project with a school or class of a different branch? If so, what?

_____

_____

_____

_____

If you checked any of these yes, answer the following:
In your opinion, was it a good idea?_____
Why or why not?

_____

_____

Did it work well, with good results?_____
Why or why not?

_____

_____

If you checked no in the boxes above, answer the following:
Why, in your opinion, has your class or school never been involved with a class from the other branches of Judaism?

_____

_____

Should it have happened?_____
Why or why not?

_____

_____

How could you or your class get started on such a project?

_____

_____

_____

_____

_____

One Prayer, Four Versions
Here's a challenge without tricks, with definite answers, definite proofs—well, almost!

Below are four versions of the prayer for peace in Jewish worship—Reform, Conservative, Orthodox, and Reconstructionist—though not necessarily in that order. Compare them carefully, then use the following "Helpful Hints" to decide how to label them: R (Reform), C (Conservative), O (Orthodox), or Rec (Reconstructionist)—a branch of Judaism that was not discussed extensively in this book. It would be a good idea for you to study it on your own.

_____ 1. Grant peace, welfare, blessing, grace, lovingkindness, and mercy unto us and unto all Thy people Israel.

_____ 2. Grant peace, well-being, and blessing unto the world, with grace, lovingkindness, and mercy for all and for all Israel Thy people.

_____ 3. Grant peace, blessing, lovingkindness, and mercy to us and to all who revere Thee.

_____ 4. Grant us peace, Thy most precious gift, O Thou eternal Source of peace, and enable Israel to be its messenger unto the peoples of the earth.

Helpful Hints:
- · Which one speaks only for the congregation and all other Jews? Label that one O.
- · Which one adds to the O prayer the idea of all humankind? Label that one C.
- · Which one speaks of having a special mission or purpose in the world? Label that one R.
- · Label the one remaining Rec. To check on your correctness: The Rec version omits the idea that Jews are a special or "chosen" people.

Yes or No?

Answer these questions by checking each YES or NO. (Be careful, some tricky ones here!)

_____ 1. Does the O version ("unto us and unto all Thy people Israel") imply that Orthodox Jews do not want peace for the entire world?

_____ 2. Do the O and C versions imply that Jews are not a special or "chosen" people?

_____ 3. Do the O, C, and Rec versions imply that God is not the source of peace?

_____ 4. Does the C version imply that Conservative Jews do not pray for the peace of their own congregation?

_____ 5. In the R, C, and O versions, does "Israel" mean the State of Israel?

_____ 6. Does the Rec version imply that Jews are just like other peoples?

_____ 7. Does the Rec version imply that Reconstructionist Jews do not pray for peace for non-Jews?

Before you take on this challenge, you should talk everything over with your classmates, your teacher, and your parents.

1. What are some common ideas, elements, terms in all four versions?

   _____

   _____

   _____

   _____

2. What are some differences between any two, three, or all four versions?

   _____

   _____

   _____

   _____

   _____

3. Are the common ideas, elements, terms:

   _____important?

   _____unimportant?

   Which is more important?

   _____the common ideas, elements, terms;

   _____the differences in ideas, elements, terms.

4. The original Hebrew version of this prayer for peace is the same in all prayer books. The translation into English is what we've been comparing. If you're a Hebrew student, check this out.

   Question: If the English "translation" is not exact but depends on a Reform or a Conservative interpretation, why not change the original Hebrew? Why keep the Hebrew at all? Try answering these questions in a class discussion, then write down the class answer—then yours, if different.

_____

_____

_____

_____

_____

5. If Reform can have a "free" translation of a prayer for peace, can we have a "free" translation that eliminates masculine language? Try your hand at that.

Facts You Should Know:

- The Reform version above is taken from the "old" *Union Prayer Book* published by the Central Conference of American Rabbis in 1940 (p. 140). It is what is called a "free" translation: not exactly what the Hebrew says, but expressing the basic idea in a more modern, more Reform way.

- In 1975, the CCAR published *Gates of Prayer: The New Union Prayer Book (Shaaray Tefillah).* Here, the "free" translation is somewhat different from the 1940 translation: "We pray for the peace of Israel and all the nations. Our prophets envisaged an age of blessing. Still we yearn for it and work for it" (p. 100).

- *Gates of Prayer* frequently uses two other prayers for peace. One reads: "O Sovereign Lord of peace, let Israel Your people know enduring peace, for it is good in Your sight continually to bless Israel with Your peace" (p. 46). The other: "May He who causes peace to reign in the high heavens let peace descend on us, on all Israel, and all the world" (p. 47).

1. This last prayer is the last paragraph of the *Kaddish*—
    which is not a prayer for the dead but a prayer in praise
    of God, recited during the worship service. So why has
    it come to be used as a mourner's prayer?

    _____

    _____

    _____

    _____

    _____

2. Compare the Hebrew for the three translations quoted
    above from *Gates of Prayer.* (For the student of He-
    brew.)

    _____

    _____

    _____

    _____

3. Carefully compare the English translations. Write down
    the conclusions you can draw from these three prayers
    about Reform Judaism's interpretations of a prayer for
    peace. Compare them with the No. 4 version above.
    Have any Reform ideas changed between 1940 and
    1975? Explain your answer.

    _____

    _____

    _____

    _____

4. Do these three prayers resemble prayers Nos. 1, 2, and 3 above? If so, how? If not, how do they differ?

_____

_____

_____

_____

_____

_____

_____

_____

_____

5. Talk your ideas over with teachers, students, and parents. Report their views.

_____

_____

_____

_____

_____

_____

_____

And now for the correct answers!
One Prayer, Four Versions: 1. Orthodox; 2. Conservative; 3. Reconstructionist; 4. Reform.
Yes or No: All no.

ROUND SEVEN

You Be the Judge

Here are some statements about the differences between Reform, Conservative, and Orthodox Judaism made by Jews from the different branches.

Your job: Pretend you are a teacher and are giving each statement a mark or grade as if it were a final test. Use any system you want—A, B, C or 100, 90, 80, etc. Explain the reason for giving such a grade.

1. The Orthodox believe in a strict interpretation of the laws and customs of their ancestors. They observe the dietary and Sabbath laws very carefully. In their synagogue the men and women sit apart, and a *minyan* (quorum of ten men) must be present before a service can take place. Their pulpit is usually in the center and they never use an organ to provide music for their religious ceremonies.

   The Conservatives are between the Orthodox and the Reform. They also observe all the holidays but not in such a strict manner. In many temples, the men and women may sit together. The sermon is usually given in English (or the language of the country), but much of the service is in Hebrew.

   Reform Jews are those who live in a modern manner and believe in loving God soulfully rather than ceremoniously. They believe in beautifying their temples. They make use of organ music and choirs to a great extent.

*Mark:*_____. I think this statement was written by a:

_____ Reform Jew;

_____ Conservative Jew;

_____ Orthodox Jew;

_____ none of these;

_____ I'm not sure.

Comment:

_____

_____

_____

_____

2. Orthodox Judaism bases its beliefs and practices upon the belief in a personal Deity who has created human beings in the divine image and, at one point in history, revealed a code of ethics and ritual to determine how for all generations the Jewish people shall live their lives.

Conservative Judaism basically rejects the concept that God gave this Torah to Moses on Mt. Sinai in favor of a historical development.

Reform Judaism rejects the ritual of this Torah in favor of general acceptance of its ethical teachings.

*Mark:*_____. I think this statement was written by a:

_____ Reform Jew;

_____ Conservative Jew;

_____ Orthodox Jew;

_____ none of these;

_____ I'm not sure.

Comment:

_____

_____

_____

_____

3. Orthodox Jews regard their faith as a tradition that has been unaltered for the past three thousand years. They accept the Bible as the revealed Word of God. They do not change with each new "wind of doctrine"; they say that their way of life yields neither to convenience nor to comfort. Orthodox Jews observe the Sabbath strictly (no work, no travel, no writing, no business dealings, no carrying of money). They observe every detail of the dietary laws. They maintain separate pews for women in the synagogue. They use only Hebrew in prayer and ceremonial services.

Reform Judaism differs sharply from Orthodoxy on the matter of revelation. Reform Jews accept as binding only the moral laws of the Bible and those ceremonies that "elevate and sanctify" our lives. They do not follow customs they believe "not adapted to the views and habits of modern civilization." Reform Jews feel that faith must be rational and able to stand up to the careful examination of reason and science. The worship of Reform Judaism departs from traditional forms. There is complete equality of the sexes in the temple. Prayer is largely in English (or the daily language). There is greater flexibility in the choice of prayers. Instrumental music is permitted in the temple. The prayer shawl *(talit)* is not worn by the male worshipers.

Conservative Jews follow the pattern of traditional Judaism, by and large, but regard Judaism as an evolving and ever-growing religion. They feel that change should be the result of natural growth and in accordance with the spirit of Jewish law. They regard Reform Judaism as a sharp break with the past. Conservative Jews follow the dietary laws, with only minor adjustments. They observe the Sabbath, High Holy Days, and festivals in traditional ways. But they have borrowed many of the forms of Reform Judaism, such as the late Friday evening service and the use of English in prayers.

*Mark:*_____. I think this statement was written by a:

_____ Reform Jew;

_____ Conservative Jew;

_____ Orthodox Jew;

_____ none of these;

_____ I'm not sure.

Comment:

_____

_____

_____

_____

4. Conservative Judaism, though rooted in tradition and accepting the traditional law, seeks within the framework of that law, both in ritual practice and day-to-day behavior, to find a way of living in the twentieth century whereby ancient wisdom and insights will help a person achieve a higher form of life.

    In the Orthodox synagogue, the men and women sit in separate sections; in the Conservative temple the men and women generally sit together; and in the Reform house of worship the men and women sit together and heads are uncovered during the services.

    Orthodox Judaism believes that God said it all at Sinai; Conservatives agree with this, but they also believe in continuing revelations. They believe in the development of rabbinic traditions as interpreted from the Bible. Conservative Judaism is not just the middle position between Orthodox and Reform.

*Mark:*_____. I think this statement was written by a:

_____ Reform Jew;

_____ Conservative Jew;

_____ Orthodox Jew;

_____ none of these;

_____ I'm not sure.

Comment:

_____

_____

_____

_____

5. It's much easier to draw a line between the Orthodox and the Reform, because the Conservatives stand somewhere between. Orthodoxy believes in the literal interpretation of the Torah and in observing its 613 commandments. It is also true, however, that Orthodoxy has had a reform element in it. Orthodoxy today is not the same as it was in the days of Moses because interpretation and reinterpretation of Torah by rabbinic courts have altered Orthodox customs. But its changes are not as frequent as Reform which believes in a constant adaptation of ancient law to modern conditions. Orthodox Jews believe in a personal Messiah and pray for a physical resurrection of the body after death. Orthodox tradition believes that, on the day the Messiah sounds the *shofar* and announces the messianic age, all the dead will be resurrected.

    Reform Judaism does not believe in physical resurrection but in some manner of spiritual immortality. Reform Judaism does not believe in a personal Messiah, but in a messianic age of peace and justice which all of us must try to bring nearer.

    As for Conservatism, it is really a reform movement, because it does believe in change and adaptation and has adopted many changes initiated by Reform.

*Mark:*_____. I think this statement was written by a:

_____ Reform Jew;

_____ Conservative Jew;

_____ Orthodox Jew;

_____ none of these;

_____ I'm not sure.

Comment:

_____

_____

_____

_____

Do most of your classmates agree with you and your grades?

_____

Does your teacher?_____

What are some good and bad points you found in these statements?

_____

_____

_____

_____

Where do they agree?

_____

_____

_____

_____

Where do they disagree?

_____

_____

_____

_____

And now let me tell you who made those statements!

No. 1: A thirteen-year-old pupil in a Reform religious school.

No. 2: An Orthodox rabbi.

No. 3:   A Reform rabbi.
No. 4:   A Conservative rabbi.
No. 5:   A Reform rabbi.

Surprised? Or did you guess any of them?

ROUND EIGHT

Think Tank

There will be an all-day *kinus* (assembly or conference) in your town for high school students in Reform, Conservative, and Orthodox religious schools. Your synagogue will be the "host" congregation; your class is in charge of planning the affair.

Your job: Organize a committee of four pupils, each to complete one of the tasks below.

Or: Organize four different committees, each to complete one of the tasks. (A committee with a specific, one-time job is called a "task force" or an "ad hoc" committee—"ad hoc" is Latin for "for this only.")

1. *Program:* What will be the central theme, topic, or problem of the *kinus?* Think of three good ones and list them in a priority order.

    a. _____
    _____

    b. _____
    _____

    c. _____
    _____

    Be ready to say why these themes and why this order. For your first-choice theme, think of three aspects or subtopics to be taken up in the morning, afternoon, and evening of the *kinus.*

    a. _____
    _____

    b. _____
    _____

c. _____
_____

Suppose you have only two sessions to plan for, which two of these three subtopics would you choose and in what order?

a. _____
_____

b. _____
_____

For only one session, which subtopic?
_____

Say why you made these various choices.
_____
_____
_____
_____

Suppose the evening session is to be social and entertaining, following morning and afternoon discussions, outline such an evening program, related to the overall theme of the day and/or the subtopics of this theme. Give one or two specific examples for each element of your program. For example, if you'll have a song session, name a few appropriate songs; do the same for other elements of your evening program.

Theme or Subtopic:
_____
_____
_____
_____

Program Elements:
_____
_____
_____
_____

2. *Arrangements:* What problems will you have with such
   a *kinus?* Dietary laws *(kashrut)* at lunch and supper?
   Yarmulkes—must everyone wear them, or should it be
   optional? What kind of dances in the social hour?
   (Among the strictly Orthodox, men and women do not
   dance together, nor do they sit together at services.)
   Others?

   How will you handle each problem?

Problem:

_____

_____

_____

_____

Solution:

_____

_____

_____

_____

Give the reason for your decision on the basis of some
general principle.

_____

_____

_____

_____

Problem:

_____

_____

_____

_____

Solution:

_____

_____

_____

_____

Reason:

_____
_____
_____
_____

Problem:

_____
_____
_____
_____

Solution:

_____
_____
_____
_____

Reason:

_____
_____
_____
_____

3. *Panel:* There will be a panel discussion involving Reform, Conservative, and Orthodox participants. Select one of the themes or subtopics developed by the program committee, or think up one of your own. Then come up with some questions on this theme or subtopic for the panel's moderator to ask: (a) all the participants; (b) the Reform participants; (c) the Conservative participants; (d) the Orthodox participants.

4. *Library:* There will be a display at the *kinus* of Jewish books, magazines, etc. What should they be?
   _____general books and magazines;
   _____school books and magazines;
   _____both.
   Select one of the themes or subtopics developed by the program committee, or make up one of your own.

Ask your librarian or principal for some catalogs and bibliographies and make a selection.

Look for material related to your chosen theme or subtopic. How will you display these books and magazines, calling attention to chapters or articles concerning the theme or subtopic?

_____

_____

How will you group your display? By:

_____Reform;

_____Conservative;

_____Orthodox;

_____different subtopics of an overall theme;

_____other. _____

_____

Now that we understand the differences and the similarities within American Judaism, is it possible and feasible for the different branches to merge? Let us look at the last unit and see if finally we can find any guidelines to help us reach a decision.

UNIT IV

One Judaism?

One Judaism? Is it possible? If possible, what has to be done for it to happen? Has it ever been tried—and, if it has, what happened? Even if it's possible—is it desirable?

It's an exciting thought—one North American Judaism combining Reform, Conservative, and Orthodox! The three branches would then stop competing and criticizing one another and would start working together for the common benefit of all.

First, let us "discount" the extreme wings within Reform and Orthodoxy. Nobody ever expects them to get together even with their own Reform or Orthodox movement, let alone with one another. A North American Judaism, if it happens, will include the broad "middle" of religious Jews, the majority in the center who can agree with one another enough to tolerate their disagreements.

The Conservatives also have two extreme wings which might refuse to compromise and work together, but it's theoretically possible that the moderates in each wing—who are the majority—could join in a single movement. There would still be quite a few differences among them, maybe even quarrels, but they could work together as a single unified movement as long as they wanted to.

Within the Republican party, for instance, members differ and disagree, sometimes quite bitterly; and so do the Democrats. Just the same, each party manages to hold together despite their internal dissensions. Frequently, Republicans and Democrats switch parties or join together to support the same candidate. Reform, Conservative, and Orthodox Judaism also consist of various subgroups. Each branch manages to hold together though members shift affiliation and subgroups break apart over disagreements.

A few years ago, the American Jewish Congress held a forum on the question, "Is religious unity possible for Jews in America?" attended by leaders of each movement.

What do you think they answered? Put YES or NO here before you read on and see what each one of the panelists said.

Reform:_____
Conservative:_____
Orthodox:_____

And now here are their answers:

The Reform speakers said that, if all three branches accepted three main principles and left customs and observances to personal or subgroup choice, then religious unity is possible for the three wings. One yes, with an if attached to it.

The Conservative representative said that, if there were a commitment of all Jews to certain concepts but acceptance of different interpretations of these concepts, it could bring all three branches together. A second yes, with an if.

The Orthodox spokesman agreed that unity on principles and concepts, with difference in observances and interpretations, could work but only under two conditions. A third yes, if. . . .

So far, we have three movement leaders agreeing that:
· Jewish religious unity would be a good thing. (Otherwise, why would they come to such a forum!)

· All three movements agree to agree on certain basic
ideas and ideals and to disagree on exactly how to
interpret them or carry them out provided all three
give up something.

Let's look into what went on still further.

The three main principles offered for religious unity by
the Reform leader were:

· Affirmation of a personal God.
· Revelation of the Torah by God to humankind.
· The central role of Oral Tradition (that is, of Jews
deciding how to change or adapt Judaism to the
changing conditions of life under new conditions).

The speaker went on to say that regarding religious observances "let God be the judge of what is acceptable," adding
that religious unity was a "foolish dream" as long as some
Jews feel they have the right to judge who are "better Jews."

The Conservative leader did not specify the number of
concepts all Jews must accept to achieve unity but gave one
example—the idea of a covenant between God and the Jewish people. As long as all three movements accept this, each
could interpret and apply it as it saw fit.

The Orthodox leader made the following two conditions for unity:

· Jews of all three movements must stop quarreling and
competing and instead seek harmony and coopera-
tion.
· Orthodox Jews cannot accept marriage and divorce
practices that do not follow traditional Jewish law.
Therefore, Reform and Conservative Jews would
have to adopt Orthodox practice in this one area or
unity would be impossible. (In *halachah,* the traditional Jewish law, violation of marriage and divorce
procedures raises questions about the legitimacy of
children, their Jewishness, their right to marry a Jew,
or inherit under a will, or be buried in a Jewish ceme-

tery.) The point here is that, whatever else the Ortho-dox might accept, they could not accept any change in these practices without giving up their basic defini-tion of a Jew and Judaism.

> Is merging possible? What has to be done—and what has experience taught us?

A small midwest town has a Reform synagogue of about one hundred members and a Conservative synagogue of about fifty members. Some of the Conservative Jews are firmly Conservative, others "lean toward" either Orthodox or Re-form. As young people grow up and move away, and older people die, both synagogues lose members. Each year, it costs the dwindling members of both synagogues more and more to maintain their building, conduct services, provide religious school instruction and adult education, support youth groups and all other synagogue programs. Members must pay ever-increasing dues. The only practical answer seems to be: merge the two synagogues into one.

You and your classmates are the rabbis, officers, parents, and teachers of the two congregations. Work out the details of the merger.

Does each member have a vote on the decision? Since

one congregation is twice as large as the other, does each member of the larger one have two votes? Are all questions settled by the two sets of officers and officials, and with what voting strength? By a special joint committee?

Record the class decision here and whether or not you personally agree with it.

The class decided that:

_____

_____

_____

_____

_____I agree;

_____I disagree;

_____I'm not sure.

What specific problems will the merger create and how will we solve them? We're only providing a sample of questions. You should add below any problems you, your classmates, or your teacher could suggest.

1. Which rabbi?
   Decision:

   _____

   _____

2. Which prayer book?
   Decision:

   _____

   _____

3. (Question): _____
   Decision:

   _____

   _____

4. (Question): _____
    Decision:

    _____
    _____
    _____

5. (Question): _____
    Decision:

    _____
    _____
    _____

If you have still more questions and decisions, use a separate sheet to list them. Then make the following your last question and give your decision.
Conflicts are bound to arise after the merger—how will we settle them?
Decision:

_____
_____
_____

How would you rate the following four solutions to the same problem?

1. Keep both buildings. Hold Friday night services in the Reform synagogue, with a Reform prayer book. Hold Sabbath morning services, with a Conservative prayer book in the Conservative synagogue. Worshipers can go to either or both.
    This solution is____good____poor, because _____

    _____
    _____

It could be applied to what other problems of merging?

_____

_____

_____

2. Keep one building. Hold Friday night services with a
   Reform prayer book. Hold Shabbat morning services
   with a Conservative prayer book. Worshipers can go to
   either or both.
   This solution is_____good_____poor, because _____

   _____

   _____

   _____

   It could be applied to what other problems of merging?

   _____

   _____

   _____

3. Keep one building. Hold separate and simultaneous services—Reform in one part of the building, Conservative
   in another, at the same time.
   This solution is_____good_____poor, because _____

   _____

   _____

   _____

   It could be applied to what other problems of merging?

   _____

   _____

   _____

4. Keep one building. Alternate Friday night services
   between Reform and Conservative prayer books, use
   the Conservative prayer book on Saturday morning,
   and have a daily *minyan* (the ten men required quorum
   for traditional worship) with the Orthodox prayer
   book.

This solution is_____good_____poor, because _____

_____

_____

_____

It could be applied to what other problems of merging?

_____

_____

_____

Can you think of any other solutions that could be applied to more of the problems of merging?

_____

_____

_____

In your own case, does it look as if a merger will work
out into a friendly, healthy, new synagogue or will it
break down again into two groups so different they
couldn't possibly work together?

Check here the conclusions your group comes to:

_____We should not merge—we cannot solve the prob-
lems.

_____We should keep meeting together until we do solve
the problems, meanwhile finding out how other
mergers have succeeded or failed, and why.

Merging two movements?

---

1. Write down what you think of the following statement
   made by an Orthodox rabbi: "A single, uniform Judaism
   in America is not possible, and if it were possible it
   would not be desirable."

What is your stand on both points?

a._____I agree_____I disagree that a single, uniform Judaism in America is impossible, because_____

_____

_____

_____

_____

b._____I agree_____I disagree that even if possible it would not be desirable, because _____

_____

_____

_____

2. Write what you think of that statement by a Reform rabbi: "There is not a particle of difference between members of Reform and Conservative congregations in terms of their religious values. . . . Most members of Reform congregations would find themselves just as comfortable if they were compelled to worship in the Conservative manner, and the reverse would be true of those who belong to Conservative synagogues. . . . Eventually the Conservative and Reform movements in the United States would find that so little divides them ideologically (in beliefs) that their separate existence would become meaningless and fruitless."

Give your stand on the two following points.

a._____I agree_____I disagree that there is no difference in religious values or beliefs, because _____

_____

_____

_____

_____

b._____I agree_____I disagree that Conservative and

Reform Jews would find themselves just as comfortable
if compelled to worship in the other's manner, because

_____

_____

_____

_____

_____

The Reform rabbi quoted above listed the various obstacles
in the way of a Reform/Conservative merger. He labelled
them as easy, harder, and hardest to overcome—religious
beliefs and values; yarmulke; prayer book; attitude on inter-
marriage; ritual observance (for example: one or two-day
holidays); attitude toward divorce; worship; attitude toward
conversion of Christians to Judaism.

Your job: Identify which ones belong in which column
below. You can also add to the list some ideas of your own
or any suggested by your classmates or your teacher.

Easy	*Harder*	*Hardest*

3. Write to the UAHC Department of Synagogue Administration, 838 Fifth Avenue, New York, NY 10021, for reports on synagogue mergers. Examine carefully these materials. Now go back over all your previous answers and decide if you still would give the same or would want to change them.

Challenge and a Final Word

We have come to the end of our book. We have been challenged. Our understanding of Judaism has been deepened. We know many of the similarities and the differences among the three branches of Judaism. But have we been able to come to a conclusion as to whether it's possible to merge or not, and if possible—is it desirable? This is the challenge that is yours. In life we don't always find easy answers to difficult questions. It's easy to make a choice between good and evil, but not so easy between two goods. It's our responsibility, though, to keep searching and investigating. Learning is a never-ending process. Rabbi Tarphon taught, "It is not incumbent upon you to complete the work but neither are you free to desist from it altogether."